MYTHS & LEGENDS
OF OUR OWN LAND
VOLUME ONE

CHARLES M. SKINNER

COSIMO CLASSICS

NEW YORK

Myths & Legends of Our Own Land - Volume One
© 2005 Cosimo, Inc.

Cosimo, P.O. Box 416
Old Chelsea Station
New York, NY 10113-0416

or visit our website at:
www.cosimobooks.com

Myths & Legends of Our Own Land - Volume One originally published by J.B. Lippincott Company in 1896.

Library of Congress Cataloging-in-Publication Data
A catalog record for this book is available from the Library of Congress

Cover design by www.wiselephant.com

ISBN: 1-59605-179-5

THESE VOLUMES,

BEING CONCERNED WITH AMERICA
AND AMERICANS,

𝕴 𝔇𝔢𝔡𝔦𝔠𝔞𝔱𝔢

TO THOSE STERLING PATRIOTS,

MY CHILDREN.

Preface

IT is unthinkingly said and often, that America is not old enough to have developed a legendary era, for such an era grows backward as a nation grows forward. No little of the charm of European travel is ascribed to the glamour that history and fable have flung around old churches, castles, and the favored haunts of tourists, and the Rhine and Hudson are frequently compared, to the prejudice of the latter, not because its scenery lacks in loveliness or grandeur, but that its beauty has not been humanized by love of chivalry or faerie, as that of the older stream has been. Yet the record of our country's progress is of deep import, and as time goes on the figures seen against the morning twilight of our history will rise to more commanding stature, and the mists of legend will invest them with a softness or glory that shall make reverence for them spontaneous and deep. Washington hurling the stone across the Potomac may live as the Siegfried of some Western saga, and Franklin invoking the lightnings may be the Loki of our mythology. The bibliography of American legends is slight, and these tales have been gathered from sources the most diverse: records, histories, newspapers, magazines, oral narrative—in every case reconstructed. The pursuit of them has been so long that a claim may be set forth for some measure of completeness.

Preface

But, whatever the episodes of our four historic centuries may furnish to the poet, painter, dramatist, or legend-building idealist of the future, it is certain that we are not devoid of myth and folk-lore. Some characters, prosaic enough, perhaps, in daily life, have impinged so lightly on society before and after perpetrating their one or two great deeds, that they have already become shadowy and their achievements have acquired a color of the supernatural. It is where myth and history combine that legend is most interesting and appeals to our fancy or our sympathy most strongly ; and it is not too early for us to begin the collation of those quaint happenings and those spoken reports that gain in picturesqueness with each transmission. An attempt has been made in this instance to assemble only legends, for, doubtful as some historians profess to find them, certain occurrences, like the story of Captain Smith and Pocahontas, and the ride of General Putnam down Breakneck Stairs, are taught as history ; while as to folk-lore, that of the Indian tribes and of the Southern negro is too copious to be recounted in this work. It will be noted that traditions do not thrive in brick and brownstone, and that the stories once rife in the colonial cities have almost as effectually disappeared as the architectural landmarks of last century. The field entered by the writer is not untrodden. Hawthorne and Irving have made paths across it, and it is hoped that others may deem its farther exploration worthy of their efforts.

Contents of Volume I

Contents of Volume I

Contents of Volume I

Contents of Volume I

Contents of Volume I

Illustrations

Volume I

The Hudson and its Hills

The Hudson and its Hills

RIP VAN WINKLE

THE story of Rip Van Winkle, told by Irving, dramatized by Boucicault, acted by Jefferson, pictured by Darley, set to music by Bristow, is the best known of American legends. Rip was a real personage, and the Van Winkles are a considerable family at this day. An idle, good-natured, happy-go-lucky fellow, he lived, presumably, in the village of Catskill, and began his long sleep in 1769. His wife was a shrew, and to escape her abuse Rip often took his dog and gun and roamed away to the Catskills, nine miles westward, where he lounged or hunted, as the humor seized him. It was on a September evening, during a jaunt on South Mountain, that he met a stubby, silent man, of goodly girth, his round head topped with a steeple hat, the skirts of his belted coat and flaps of his petticoat trousers meeting at the tops of heavy boots, and the face—ugh!—green and ghastly, with unmoving eyes that glimmered in the twilight like phosphorus. The dwarf carried a keg, and on receiving an intimation, in a sign, that he would like Rip to relieve him of it, that cheerful vagabond shouldered it and marched on up the mountain.

Myths and Legends

At nightfall they emerged on a little plateau where a score of men in the garb of long ago, with faces like that of Rip's guide, and equally still and speechless, were playing bowls with great solemnity, the balls sometimes rolling over the plateau's edge and rumbling down the rocks with a boom like thunder. A cloaked and snowy-bearded figure, watching aloof, turned like the others, and gazed uncomfortably at the visitor who now came blundering in among them. Rip was at first for making off, but the sinister glare in the circle of eyes took the run out of his legs, and he was not displeased when they signed to him to tap the keg and join in a draught of the ripest schnapps that ever he had tasted,—and he knew the flavor of every brand in Catskill. While these strange men grew no more genial with passing of the flagons, Rip was pervaded by a satisfying glow; then, overcome by sleepiness and resting his head on a stone, he stretched his tired legs out and fell to dreaming.

Morning. Sunlight and leaf shadow were dappled over the earth when he awoke, and rising stiffly from his bed, with compunctions in his bones, he reached for his gun. The already venerable implement was so far gone with rot and rust that it fell to pieces in his hand, and looking down at the fragments of it, he saw that his clothes were dropping from his body in rags and mould, while a white beard flowed over his breast. Puzzled and alarmed, shaking his head ruefully as he recalled the carouse

The Hudson and its Hills

of the silent, he hobbled down the mountain as fast as he might for the grip of the rheumatism on his knees and elbows, and entered his native village. What! Was this Catskill? Was this the place that he left yesterday? Had all these houses sprung up overnight, and these streets been pushed across the meadows in a day? The people, too: where were his friends? The children who had romped with him, the rotund topers whom he had left cooling their hot noses in pewter pots at the tavern door, the dogs that used to bark a welcome, recognizing in him a kindred spirit of vagrancy: where were they?

And his wife, whose athletic arm and agile tongue had half disposed him to linger in the mountains: how happened it that she was not awaiting him at the gate? But gate there was none in the familiar place: an unfenced yard of weeds and ruined foundation wall were there. Rip's home was gone. The idlers jeered at his bent, lean form, his snarl of beard and hair, his disreputable dress, his look of grieved astonishment. He stopped, instinctively, at the tavern, for he knew that place in spite of its new sign: an officer in blue regimentals and a cocked hat replacing the crimson George III. of his recollection, and labelled "General Washington." There was a quick gathering of ne'er-do-weels, of tavern-haunters and gaping 'prentices, about him, and though their faces were strange and their manners rude, he made bold to ask if they knew such and such of his friends.

"Nick Vedder? He's dead and gone these eighteen years." "Brom Dutcher? He joined the army and was killed at Stony Point." "Van Brummel? He, too, went to the war, and is in Congress now."

"And Rip Van Winkle?"

"Yes, he's here. That's him yonder."

And to Rip's utter confusion he saw before him a counterpart of himself, as young, lazy, ragged, and easy-natured as he remembered himself to be, yesterday—or, was it yesterday?

"That's young Rip," continued his informer. "His father was Rip Van Winkle, too, but he went to the mountains twenty years ago and never came back. He probably fell over a cliff, or was carried off by Indians, or eaten by bears."

Twenty years ago! Truly, it was so. Rip had slept for twenty years without awaking. He had left a peaceful colonial village; he returned to a bustling republican town. How he eventually found, among the oldest inhabitants, some who admitted that they knew him; how he found a comfortable home with his married daughter and the son who took after him so kindly; how he recovered from the effect of the tidings that his wife had died of apoplexy, in a quarrel; how he resumed his seat at the tavern tap and smoked long pipes and told long yarns for the rest of his days, were matters of record up to the beginning of this century.

And a strange story Rip had to tell, for he had served as cup-bearer to the dead crew of the Half

The Hudson and its Hills

Moon. He had quaffed a cup of Hollands with no
other than Henry Hudson himself. Some say that
Hudson's spirit has made its home amid these hills,
that it may look into the lovely valley that he discovered; but others hold that every twenty years he
and his men assemble for a revel in the mountains
that so charmed them when first seen swelling against
the western heavens, and the liquor they drink on
this night has the bane of throwing any mortal who
lips it into a slumber whence nothing can arouse him
until the day dawns when the crew shall meet again.
As you climb the east front of the mountains by the
old carriage road, you pass, half-way up the height,
the stone that Rip Van Winkle slept on, and may see
that it is slightly hollowed by his form. The ghostly
revellers are due in the Catskills in 1909, and let all
tourists who are among the mountains in September
of that year beware of accepting liquor from strangers.

CATSKILL GNOMES

BEHIND the New Grand Hotel, in the Catskills,
is an amphitheatre of mountain that is held to
be the place of which the Mohicans spoke when they
told of people there who worked in metals, and had
bushy beards and eyes like pigs. From the smoke
of their forges, in autumn, came the haze of Indian
summer; and when the moon was full, it was their
custom to assemble on the edge of a precipice above
the hollow and dance and caper until the night was

nigh worn away. They brewed a liquor that had the effect of shortening the bodies and swelling the heads of all who drank it, and when Hudson and his crew visited the mountains, the pygmies held a carouse in his honor and invited him to drink their liquor. The crew went away, shrunken and distorted by the magic distillation, and thus it was that Rip Van Winkle found them on the eve of his famous sleep.

THE CATSKILL WITCH

WHEN the Dutch gave the name of Katzbergs to the mountains west of the Hudson, by reason of the wild-cats and panthers that ranged there, they obliterated the beautiful Indian Ontiora, "mountains of the sky." In one tradition of the red men these hills were bones of a monster that fed on human beings until the Great Spirit turned it into stone as it was floundering toward the ocean to bathe. The two lakes near the summit were its eyes. These peaks were the home of an Indian witch, who adjusted the weather for the Hudson Valley with the certainty of a signal service bureau. It was she who let out the day and night in blessed alternation, holding back the one when the other was at large, for fear of conflict. Old moons she cut into stars as soon as she had hung new ones in the sky, and she was often seen perched on Round Top and North Mountain, spinning clouds and flinging them to the

The Hudson and its Hills

winds. Woe betide the valley residents if they
showed irreverence, for then the clouds were black
and heavy, and through them she poured floods of
rain and launched the lightnings, causing disastrous
freshets in the streams and blasting the wigwams of
the mockers. In a frolic humor she would take the
form of a bear or deer and lead the Indian hunters
anything but a merry dance, exposing them to tire
and peril, and vanishing or assuming some terrible
shape when they had overtaken her. Sometimes she
would lead them to the cloves and would leap into
the air with a mocking " Ho, ho!" just as they
stopped with a shudder at the brink of an abyss.
Garden Rock was a spot where she was often found,
and at its foot a lake once spread. This was held
in such awe that an Indian would never wittingly
pursue his quarry there ; but once a hunter lost his
way and emerged from the forest at the edge of the
pond. Seeing a number of gourds in crotches of the
trees he took one, but fearing the spirit he turned to
leave so quickly that he stumbled and it fell. As it
broke, a spring welled from it in such volume that the
unhappy man was gulfed in its waters, swept to the
edge of Kaaterskill clove and dashed on the rocks
two hundred and sixty feet below. Nor did the
water ever cease to run, and in these times the
stream born of the witch's revenge is known as
Catskill Creek.

Myths and Legends

THE REVENGE OF SHANDAKEN

ON the rock platform where the Catskill Mountain House now stands, commanding one of the fairest views in the world, old chief Shandaken set his wigwam,—for it is a mistake to suppose that barbarians are indifferent to beauty,—and there his daughter, Lotowana, was sought in marriage by his braves. She, however, kept faith to an early vow exchanged with a young chief of the Mohawks. A suitor who was particularly troublesome was Norsereddin, proud, morose, dark-featured, a stranger to the red man, a descendant, so he claimed, from Egyptian kings, and who lived by himself on Kaaterskill Creek, appearing among white settlements but rarely.

On one of his visits to Catskill, a tavern-lounging Dutchman wagered him a thousand golden crowns that he could not win Lotowana, and, stung by avarice as well as inflamed by passion, Norsereddin laid new siege to her heart. Still the girl refused to listen, and Shandaken counselled him to be content with the smiles of others, thereby so angering the Egyptian that he assailed the chief and was driven from the camp with blows; but on the day of Lotowana's wedding with the Mohawk he returned, and in a honeyed speech asked leave to give a jewel to the bride to show that he had stifled jealousy and ill will. The girl took the handsome box he gave her and drew the cover, when a spring flew forward, driving into her hand the poisoned tooth of a snake that had been affixed to it. The venom was strong, and in a few minutes Lotowana lay dead at her husband's feet.

Though the Egyptian had disappeared into the forest directly on the acceptance of his treacherous gift, twenty braves set off in pursuit, and overtaking him on the Kalkberg, they dragged him back to the rock where father and husband were bewailing the maid's untimely fate. A pile of fagots was heaped within a few feet of the precipice edge, and tying their captive on them, they applied the torch, dancing about with cries of exultation as the shrieks of the wretch echoed from the cliffs. The dead girl was buried by the mourning tribe, while the ashes of Norsereddin were left to be blown abroad. On the day of his revenge Shandaken left his ancient dwelling-place, and his camp-fires never glimmered afterward on the front of Ontiora.

CONDEMNED TO THE NOOSE

RALPH SUTHERLAND, who, early in the last century, occupied a stone house a mile from Leeds, in the Catskills, was a man of morose and violent disposition, whose servant, a Scotch girl, was virtually a slave, inasmuch as she was bound to work for him without pay until she had refunded to him her passage-money to this country. Becoming weary of bondage and of the tempers of her mas-

ter, the girl ran away. The man set off in a raging
chase, and she had not gone far before Sutherland
overtook her, tied her by the wrists to his horse's
tail, and began the homeward journey. Afterward,
he swore that the girl stumbled against the horse's
legs, so frightening the animal that it rushed off
madly, pitching him out of the saddle and dashing the servant to death on rocks and trees; yet,
knowing how ugly-tempered he could be, his neighbors were better inclined to believe that he had
driven the horse into a gallop, intending to drag the
girl for a short distance, as a punishment, and to
rein up before he had done serious mischief. On
this supposition he was arrested, tried, and sentenced
to die on the scaffold.

The tricks of circumstantial evidence, together
with pleas advanced by influential relatives of the
prisoner, induced the court to delay sentence until
the culprit should be ninety-nine years old, but it
was ordered that, while released on his own recog-
nizance, in the interim, he should keep a hangman's
noose about his neck and show himself before the
judges in Catskill once every year, to prove that he
wore his badge of infamy and kept his crime in
mind. This sentence he obeyed, and there were
people living recently who claimed to remember
him as he went about with a silken cord knotted at
his throat. He was always alone, he seldom spoke,
his rough, imperious manner had departed. Only
when children asked him what the rope was for

were his lips seen to quiver, and then he would hurry away. After dark his house was avoided, for gossips said that a shrieking woman passed it nightly, tied at the tail of a giant horse with fiery eyes and smoking nostrils; that a skeleton in a winding sheet had been found there; that a curious thing, somewhat like a woman, had been known to sit on his garden wall, with lights shining from her finger-tips, uttering unearthly laughter; and that domestic animals reproached the man by groaning and howling beneath his windows.

These beliefs he knew, yet he neither grieved, nor scorned, nor answered when he was told of them. Years sped on. Every year deepened his reserve and loneliness, and some began to whisper that he would take his own way out of the world, though others answered that men who were born to be hanged would never be drowned; but a new republic was created; new laws were made; new judges sat to minister them; so, on Ralph Sutherland's ninety-ninth birthday anniversary, there were none who would accuse him or execute sentence. He lived yet another year, dying in 1801. But was it from habit, or was it in self-punishment and remorse, that he never took off the cord? for, when he drew his last breath, though it was in his own house, his throat was still encircled by the hangman's rope.

Myths and Legends

BIG INDIAN

INTERMARRIAGES between white people and red ones in this country were not uncommon in the days when our ancestors led as rude a life as the natives, and several places in the Catskills commemorate this fact. Mount Utsayantha, for example, is named for an Indian woman whose life, with that of her baby and her white husband, was lost there. For the white men early found friends among these mountains. As far back as 1663 they spared Catherine Dubois and her three children, after some rash spirits had abducted them and carried them to a place on the upper Walkill, to do them to death; for the captives raised a Huguenot hymn and the hearts of their captors were softened.

In Esopus Valley lived Winnisook, whose height was seven feet, and who was known among the white settlers as "the big Indian." He loved a white girl of the neighborhood, one Gertrude Molyneux, and had asked for her hand; but while she was willing, the objections of her family were too strong to be overcome, and she was teased into marriage with Joseph Bundy, of her own race, instead. She liked the Indian all the better after that, however, because Bundy proved to be a bad fellow, and believing that she could be happier among barbarians than among a people that approved such marriages, she eloped with Winnisook. For a long time all trace of the runaway couple was lost, but one day the man having gone down to the plain to steal cattle, it was alleged, was discovered by some farmers who knew him, and who gave hot chase, coming up with him at the place now called Big Indian.

Foremost in the chase was Bundy. As he came near to the enemy of his peace he exclaimed, "I think the best way to civilize that yellow serpent is to let daylight into his heart," and, drawing his rifle to his shoulder, he fired. Mortally wounded, yet instinctively seeking refuge, the giant staggered into the hollow of a pine-tree, where the farmers lost sight of him. There, however, he was found by Gertrude, bolt upright, yet dead. The unwedded widow brought her dusky children to the place and spent the remainder of her days near his grave. Until a few years ago the tree was still pointed out, but a railroad company has now covered it with an embankment.

THE BAKER'S DOZEN

BAAS [BOSS] VOLCKERT JAN PIETER-SEN VAN AMSTERDAM kept a bake-shop in Albany, and lives in history as the man who invented New Year cakes and made gingerbread babies in the likeness of his own fat offspring. Good churchman though he was, the bane of his life was a fear of being bewitched, and perhaps it was to keep out evil spirits, who might make one last effort to gain the mastery over him, ere he turned the customary leaf

with the incoming year, that he had primed himself
with an extra glass of spirits on the last night of 1654.
His sales had been brisk, and as he sat in his little
shop, meditating comfortably on the gains he would
make when his harmless rivals—the knikkerbakkers
(bakers of marbles)—sent for their usual supply of
olie-koeks and mince-pies on the morrow, he was
startled by a sharp rap, and an ugly old woman entered. "Give me a dozen New Year's cookies!"
she cried, in a shrill voice.

"Vell, den, you needn' sbeak so loud. I aind
teaf, den."

"A dozen!" she screamed. "Give me a dozen.
Here are only twelve."

"Vell, den, dwalf is a dozen."

"One more! I want a dozen."

"Vell, den, if you vant anodder, go to de duyvil
and ged it."

Did the hag take him at his word? She left the
shop, and from that time it seemed as if poor
Volckert was bewitched, indeed, for his cakes were
stolen; his bread was so light that it went up the
chimney, when it was not so heavy that it fell
through the oven; invisible hands plucked bricks
from that same oven and pelted him until he was
blue; his wife became deaf, his children went un-
kempt, and his trade went elsewhere. Thrice the
old woman reappeared, and each time was sent anew
to the devil; but at last, in despair, the baker called
on Saint Nicolaus to come and advise him. His call

was answered with startling quickness, for, almost while he was making it, the venerable patron of Dutch feasts stood before him. The good soul advised the trembling man to be more generous in his dealings with his fellows, and after a lecture on charity he vanished, when, lo! the old woman was there in his place.

She repeated her demand for one more cake, and Volckert Jan Pietersen, etc., gave it, whereupon she exclaimed, "The spell is broken, and from this time a dozen is thirteen!" Taking from the counter a gingerbread effigy of Saint Nicolaus, she made the astonished Dutchman lay his hand upon it and swear to give more liberal measure in the future. So, until thirteen new States arose from the ruins of the colonies,—when the shrewd Yankees restored the original measure,—thirteen made a baker's dozen.

THE DEVIL'S DANCE-CHAMBER.

MOST storied of our New World rivers is the Hudson. Historic scenes have been enacted on its shores, and Indian, Dutchman, Briton, and American have invested it with romance. It had its source, in the red man's fancy, in a spring of eternal youth; giants and spirits dwelt in its woods and hills, and before the river—Shatemuc, king of streams, the red men called it—had broken through the highlands, those mountains were a pent for spirits who had rebelled against the Manitou.

31

Myths and Legends

After the waters had forced a passage to the sea these evil ones sought shelter in the glens and valleys that open to right and left along its course, but in time of tempest, when they hear Manitou riding down the ravine on wings of storm, dashing thunderbolts against the cliffs, it is the fear that he will recapture them and force them into lightless caverns to expiate their revolt, that sends them huddling among the rocks and makes the hills resound with roars and howls.

At the Devil's Dance-Chamber, a slight plateau on the west bank, between Newburg and Crom Elbow, the red men performed semi-religious rites as a preface to their hunting and fishing trips or ventures on the war-path. They built a fire, painted themselves, and in that frenzy into which savages are so readily lashed, and that is so like to the action of mobs in trousers, they tumbled, leaped, danced, yelled, sang, grimaced, and gesticulated until the Manitou disclosed himself, either as a harmless animal or a beast of prey. If he came in the former shape the augury was favorable, but if he showed himself as a bear or panther, it was a warning of evil that they seldom dared to disregard.

The crew of Hudson's ship, the Half Moon, having chanced on one of these orgies, were so impressed by the fantastic spectacle that they gave the name Duyvels Dans-Kamer to the spot. Years afterwards, when Stuyvesant ascended the river, his doughty retainers were horrified, on landing below

the Dans-Kamer, to discover hundreds of painted
figures frisking there in the fire-light. A few surmised that they were but a new generation of savages holding a powwow, but most of the sailors
fancied that the assemblage was demoniac, and that
the figures were spirits of bad Indians repeating a
scalp-dance and revelling in the mysterious fire-water
that they had brought down from the river source
in jars and skins. The spot was at least once pro-
faned with blood, for a young Dutchman and his
wife, of Albany, were captured here by an angry
Indian, and although the young man succeeded in
stabbing his captor to death, he was burned alive on
the rock by the friends of the Indian whose wrath
he had provoked. The wife, after being kept in
captivity for a time, was ransomed.

THE CULPRIT FAY

THE wood-tick's drum convokes the elves at the
noon of night on Cro' Nest top, and, clam-
bering out of their flower-cup beds and hammocks of
cobweb, they fly to the meeting, not to freak about the
grass or banquet at the mushroom table, but to hear
sentence passed on the fay who, forgetting his vestal
vow, has loved an earthly maid. From his throne
under a canopy of tulip petals, borne on pillars of
shell, the king commands silence, and with severe
eye but softened voice he tells the culprit that while
he has scorned the royal decree he has saved himself

3

from the extreme penalty, of imprisonment in wal-
nut shells and cobweb dungeons, by loving a maid
who is gentle and pure. So it shall be enough if he
will go down to the Hudson and seize a drop from
the bow of mist that a sturgeon leaves when he
makes his leap; and after, to kindle his darkened
flame-wood lamp at a meteor spark. The fairy
bows, and without a word slowly descends the rocky
steep, for his wing is soiled and has lost its power;
but once at the river, he tugs amain at a mussel shell
till he has it afloat; then, leaping in, he paddles
out with a strong grass blade till he comes to the
spot where the sturgeon swims, though the water-
sprites plague him and toss his boat, and the fish
and the leeches bunt and drag; but, suddenly, the
sturgeon shoots from the water, and ere the arch of
mist that he tracks through the air has vanished, the
sprite has caught a drop of the spray in a tiny blossom, and in this he washes clean his wings.

The water-goblins torment him no longer. They
push his boat to the shore, where, alighting, he
kisses his hand, then, even as a bubble, he flies back
to the mountain top, dons his acorn helmet, his
corselet of bee-hide, his shield of lady-bug shell,
and grasping his lance, tipped with wasp sting, he be-
strides his fire-fly steed and off he goes like a flash.
The world spreads out and then grows small, but he
flies straight on. The ice-ghosts leer from the topmost clouds, and the mists surge round, but he
shakes his lance and pipes his call, and at last he

comes to the Milky Way, where the sky-sylphs
lead him to their queen, who lies couched in a
palace ceiled with stars, its dome held up by northern lights and the curtains made of the morning's
flush. Her mantle is twilight purple, tied with
threads of gold from the eastern dawn, and her face
is as fair as the silver moon.

She begs the fay to stay with her and taste forever
the joys of heaven, but the knightly elf keeps down
the beating of his heart, for he remembers a face on
earth that is fairer than hers, and he begs to go.
With a sigh she fits him a car of cloud, with the
fire-fly steed chained on behind, and he hurries
away to the northern sky whence the meteor comes,
with roar and whirl, and as it passes it bursts to
flame. He lights his lamp at a glowing spark, then
wheels away to the fairy-land. His king and his
brothers hail him stoutly, with song and shout, and
feast and dance, and the revel is kept till the eastern
sky has a ruddy streak. Then the cock crows shrill
and the fays are gone.

POKEPSIE

THE name of this town has forty-two spellings
in old records, and with singular pertinacity
in ill-doing, the inhabitants have fastened on it the
longest and clumsiest of all. It comes from the
Mohegan words Apo-keep-sink, meaning a safe,
pleasant harbor. Harbor it might be for canoes,

but for nothing bigger, for it was only the little cove that was so called between Call Rock and Adder Cliff,—the former indicating where settlers awaiting passage hailed the masters of vessels from its top, and the latter taking its name from the snakes that abounded there.

Hither came a band of Delawares with Pequot captives, among them a young chief to whom had been offered not only life but leadership if he would renounce his tribe, receive the mark of the turtle on his breast, and become a Delaware. On his refusal, he was bound to a tree, and was about to undergo the torture, when a girl among the listeners sprang to his side. She, too, was a Pequot, but the turtle totem was on her bosom, and when she begged his life, because they had been betrothed, the captors paused to talk of it. She had chosen well the time to interfere, for a band of Hurons was approaching, and even as the talk went on their yell was heard in the wood. Instant measures for defence were taken, and in the fight that followed both chief and maiden were forgotten ; but though she cut the cords that bound him, they were separated in the confusion, he disappearing, she falling captive to the Hurons, who, sated with blood, retired from the field. In the fantastic disguise of a wizard the young Pequot entered their camp soon after, and on being asked to try his enchantments for the cure of a young woman, he entered her tent, showing no surprise at finding her to be the maiden of his choice, who was suffering from nothing worse than nerves, due to the excitement of the battle. Left alone with his patient, he disclosed his identity, and planned a way of escape that proved effective on that very night, for, though pursued by the angry Hurons, the couple reached "safe harbor," thence making a way to their own country in the east, where they were married.

DUNDERBERG

DUNDERBERG, "Thunder Mountain," at the southern gate of the Hudson Highlands, is a wooded eminence, chiefly populated by a crew of imps of stout circumference, whose leader, the Heer, is a bulbous goblin clad in the dress worn by Dutch colonists two centuries ago, and carrying a speaking-trumpet, through which he bawls his orders for the blowing of winds and the touching off of lightnings. These orders are given in Low Dutch, and are put into execution by the imps aforesaid, who troop into the air and tumble about in the mist, sometimes smiting the flag or topsail of a ship to ribbons, or laying the vessel over before the wind until she is in peril of going on beam ends. At one time a sloop passing the Dunderberg had nearly foundered, when the crew discovered the sugar-loaf hat of the Heer at the mast-head. None dared to climb for it, and it was not until she had driven past Pollopel's Island—the limit of the Heer's jurisdiction—that she righted. As she did so the little hat spun into the air like a

37

top, creating a vortex that drew up the storm-clouds, and the sloop kept her way prosperously for the rest of the voyage. The captain had nailed a horse-shoe to the mast. The " Hat Rogue" of the Devil's Bridge in Switzerland must be a relative of this gamesome sprite, for his mischief is usually of a harmless sort; but, to be on the safe side, the Dutchmen who plied along the river lowered their peaks in homage to the keeper of the mountain, and for years this was a common practice. Mariners who paid this courtesy to the Heer of the Donder Berg were never molested by his imps, though skipper Ouselsticker, of Fish-kill,—for all he had a parson on board,—was once beset by a heavy squall, and the goblin came out of the mist and sat astraddle of his bowsprit, seeming to guide his schooner straight toward the rocks. The dominie chanted the song of Saint Nicolaus, and the goblin, unable to endure either its spiritual potency or the worthy parson's singing, shot upward like a ball and rode off on the gale, carrying with him the nightcap of the parson's wife, which he hung on the weathercock of Esopus steeple, forty miles away.

ANTHONY'S NOSE

THE Hudson Highlands are suggestively named : Bear Mountain, Sugar Loaf, Cro' Nest, Storm King, called by the Dutch Boterberg, or Butter Hill, from its likeness to a pat of butter; Beacon

The Hudson and its Hills

Hill, where the fires blazed to tell the country that the Revolutionary war was over; Dunderberg, Mount Taurus, so called because a wild bull that had terrorized the Highlands was chased out of his haunts on this height, and was killed by falling from a cliff on an eminence to the northward, known, in consequence, as Breakneck Hill. These, with Anthony's Nose, are the principal points of interest in the lovely and impressive panorama that unfolds before the view as the boats fly onward.

Concerning the last-named elevation, the aquiline promontory that abuts on the Hudson opposite Dunderberg, it takes title from no resemblance to the human feature, but is so named because Anthony Van Corlaer, the trumpeter, who afterwards left a reason for calling the upper boundary of Manhattan Island Spuyten Duyvil Creek, killed the first sturgeon ever eaten at the foot of this mountain. It happened in this wise : By assiduous devotion to keg and flagon Anthony had begotten a nose that was the wonder and admiration of all who knew it, for its size was prodigious ; in color it rivalled the carbuncle, and it shone like polished copper. As Anthony was lounging over the quarter of Peter Stuyvesant's galley one summer morning this nose caught a ray from the sun and reflected it hissing into the water, where it killed a sturgeon that was rising beside the vessel. The fish was pulled aboard, eaten, and declared good, though the singed place savored of brimstone, and in commemoration of the event Stuyvesant dubbed the mountain that rose above his vessel Anthony's Nose.

MOODUA CREEK

MOODUA is an evolution, through Murdy's and Moodna, from Murderer's Creek, its present inexpressive name having been given to it by N. P. Willis. One Murdock lived on its shore with his wife, two sons, and a daughter; and often in the evening Naoman, a warrior of a neighboring tribe, came to the cabin, caressed the children, and shared the woodman's hospitality. One day the little girl found in the forest an arrow wrapped in snake-skin and tipped with crow's feather; then the boy found a hatchet hanging by a hair from a bough above the door; then a glare of evil eyes was caught for an instant in a thicket. Naoman, when he came, was reserved and stern, finding voice only to warn the family to fly that night; so, when all was still, the threatened family made its way softly, but quickly, to the Hudson shore, and embarked for Fisher's Kill, across the river.

The wind lagged and their boat drew heavily, and when, from the shade of Pollopel's Island, a canoe swept out, propelled by twelve men, the hearts of the people in the boat sank in despair. The wife was about to leap over, but Murdock drew her back; then, loading and firing as fast as possible, he laid six of his pursuers low; but the canoe was savagely urged forward, and in another minute every member of the family was a helpless captive. When the skiff had been dragged back, the prisoners were marched through the wood to an open spot where the principal members of the tribe sat in council.

The sachem arose, twisted his hands in the woman's golden hair, bared his knife, and cried, " Tell us what Indian warned you and betrayed his tribe, or you shall see husband and children bleed before your eyes." The woman answered never a word, but after a little Naoman arose and said, " 'Twas I ;" then drew his blanket about him and knelt for execution. An axe cleft his skull. Drunk with the sight of blood, the Indians rushed upon the captives and slew them, one by one. The prisoners neither shrank nor cried for mercy, but met their end with hymns upon their lips, and, seeing that they could so meet death, one member of the band let fall his arm and straight became a Christian. The cabin was burned, the bodies flung into the stream, and the stain of blood was seen for many a year in Murderer's Creek.

A TRAPPER'S GHASTLY VENGEANCE

ABOUT a mile back from the Hudson, at Coxsackie, stood the cabin of Nick Wolsey, who, in the last century, was known to the river settlements as a hunter and trapper of correct aim, shrewdness, endurance, and taciturn habit. For many years he lived in this cabin alone, except for the company of his dog; but while visiting a camp of Indians in the wilderness he was struck with the engaging manner of one of the girls of the tribe; he repeated the visit; he found cause to go to the camp frequently; he made presents to the father of the maid, and at length won her consent to be his wife. The simple marriage ceremony of the tribe was performed, and Wolsey led Minamee to his home; but the wedding was interrupted in an almost tragic manner, for a surly fellow who had loved the girl, yet who never had found courage to declare himself, was wrought to such a jealous fury at the discovery of Wolsey's good fortune that he sprang at him with a knife, and would have despatched him on the spot had not the white man's faithful hound leaped at his throat and borne him to the ground.

Wolsey disarmed the fellow and kicked and cuffed him to the edge of the wood, while the whole company shouted with laughter at this ignominious punishment, and approved it. A year or more passed. Wolsey and his Indian wife were happy in their free and simple life; happy, too, in their little babe. Wolsey was seldom absent from his cabin for any considerable length of time, and usually returned to it before the night set in. One evening he noticed that the grass and twigs were bent near his house by some passing foot that, with the keen

eye of the woodman, he saw was not his wife's.
" Some hunter," he said, " saw the house when he
passed here, and as, belike, he never saw one before,
he stopped to look in." For the trail led to his
window, and diverged thence to the forest again.
A few days later, as he was returning, he came on
the footprints that were freshly made, and a shadow
crossed his face. On nearing the door he stumbled
on the body of his dog, lying rigid on the ground.
" How did this happen, Minamee ?" he cried, as
he flung open the door. The wife answered, in a
low voice, " Hush ! you'll wake the child."

Nick Wolsey entered the cabin and stood as one
turned to marble. Minamee, his wife, sat on the
cold hearth, her face and hands cut and blackened,
her dress torn, her eyes glassy, a meaningless smile
on her lips. In her arms she pressed the body of
her infant, its dress soaked with blood, and the head
of the little creature lay on the floor beside her.
She crooned softly over the cold clay as if hushing
it to sleep, and when Wolsey at length found words,
she only whispered, " Hush ! you will wake him."
The night went heavily on ; day dawned, and the
crooning became lower and lower ; still, through all
that day the bereft woman rocked to and fro upon
the floor, and the agonized husband hung about her,
trying in vain to give comfort, to bind her wounds,
to get some explanation of the mystery that con-
fronted him. The second night set in, and it was
evident that it would be the last for Minamee. Her

strength failed until she allowed herself to be placed
on a couch of skins, while the body of her child
was gently lifted from her arms. Then, for a few
brief minutes, her reason was restored, and she
found words to tell her husband how the Indian
whose murderous attack he had thwarted at the
wedding had come to the cabin, shot the dog that
had rushed out to defend the place, beat the woman
back from the door, tore the baby from its bed,
slashed its head off with a knife, and, flinging the
little body into her lap, departed with the words,
"This is my revenge. I am satisfied." Before the
sun was in the east again Minamee was with her
baby.

Wolsey sat for hours in the ruin of his happiness, his breathing alone proving that he was alive,
and when at last he arose and went out of the house,
there were neither tears nor outcry ; he saddled his
horse and rode off to the westward. At nightfall he
came to the Indian village where he had won his
wife, and relating to the assembled tribe what had
happened, he demanded that the murderer be given
up to him. His demand was readily granted, whereupon the white man advanced on the cowering
wretch, who had confidently expected the protection
of his people, and with the quick fling and jerk of
a raw-hide rope bound his arms to his side. Then
casting a noose about his neck and tying the end of
it to his saddle-bow, he set off for the Hudson.
All that night he rode, the Indian walking and run-

ning at the horse's heels, and next day he reached his cabin. Tying his prisoner to a tree, the trapper cut a quantity of young willows, from which he fashioned a large cradle-like receptacle; in this he placed the culprit, face upward, and tied so stoutly that he could not move a finger; then going into his house, he emerged with the body of Minamee, and laid it, face downward, on the wretch, who could not repress a groan of horror as the awful burden sank on his breast. Wolsey bound together the living and the dead, and with a swing of his powerful arms he flung them on his horse's back, securing them there with so many turns of rope that nothing could displace them. Now he began to lash his horse until the poor beast trembled with anger and pain, when, flinging off the halter, he gave it a final lash, and the animal plunged, foaming and snorting, into the wilderness. When it had vanished and the hoof-beats were no longer heard, Nick Wolsey took his rifle on his arm and left his home forever. And tradition says that the horse never stopped in its mad career, but that on still nights it can be heard sweeping through the woods along the Hudson and along the Mohawk like a whirlwind, and that as the sound goes by a smothered voice breaks out in cursing, in appeal, then in harsh and dreadful laughter.

Myths and Legends

THE VANDERDECKEN OF TAPPAN ZEE

IT is Saturday night; the swell of the Hudson lazily heaves against the shores of Tappan Zee, the cliff above Tarrytown where the white lady cries on winter nights is pale in starlight, and crickets chirp in the boskage. It is so still that the lap of oars can be heard coming across the water at least a mile away. Some small boat, evidently, but of heavy build, for it takes a vigorous hand to propel it, and now there is a grinding of oars on thole-pins. Strange that it is not yet seen, for the sound is near. Look! Is that a shadow crossing that wrinkle of starlight in the water? The oars have stopped, and there is no wind to make that sound of a sigh.

Ho, Rambout Van Dam! Is it you? Are you still expiating your oath to pull from Kakiat to Spuyten Duyvil before the dawn of Sabbath, if it takes you a month of Sundays? Better for you had you passed the night with your roistering friends at Kakiat, or started homeward earlier, for Sabbath-breaking is no sin now, and you, poor ghost, will find little sympathy for your plight. Grant that your month of Sundays, or your cycle of months of Sundays, be soon up, for it is sad to be reminded that we may be punished for offences many years forgotten. When the sun is high to-morrow a score of barges will vex the sea of Tappan, each crowded with men and maids from New Amsterdam, jigging to profane music and refreshing themselves with

46

The Hudson and its Hills

such liquors as you, Rambout, never even smelled—
be thankful for that much. If your shade sits blink-
ing at them from the wooded buttresses of the Palisades, you must repine, indeed, at the hardness of
your fate.

THE GALLOPING HESSIAN

IN the flower-gemmed cemetery of Tarrytown,
where gentle Irving sleeps, a Hessian soldier
was interred after sustaining misfortune in the loss
of his head in one of the Revolutionary battles.
For a long time after he was buried it was the habit
of this gentleman to crawl from his grave at un-
seemly hours and gallop about the country, sending
shivers through the frames of many worthy people,
who shrank under their blankets when they heard
the rush of hoofs along the unlighted roads.

In later times there lived in Tarrytown—so
named because of the tarrying habits of Dutch gossips on market days, though some hard-minded people insist that Tarwe-town means Wheat-town—
a gaunt schoolmaster, one Ichabod Crane, who
cherished sweet sentiments for Katrina Van Tassell,
the buxom daughter of a farmer, also a famous maker
of pies and doughnuts. Ichabod had been calling
late one evening, and, his way home being long,
Katrina's father lent him a horse to make the journey; but even with this advantage the youth set out
with misgivings, for he had to pass the graveyard.

Myths and Legends

As it was near the hour when the Hessian was to ride, he whistled feebly to keep his courage up, but when he came to the dreaded spot the whistle died in a gasp, for he heard the tread of a horse. On looking around, his hair bristled and his heart came up like a plug in his throat to hinder his breathing, for he saw a headless horseman coming over the ridge behind him, blackly defined against the starry sky. Setting spurs to his nag with a hope of being first to reach Sleepy Hollow bridge, which the spectre never passed, the unhappy man made the best possible time in that direction, for his follower was surely overtaking him. Another minute and the bridge would be reached; but, to Ichabod's horror, the Hessian dashed alongside and, rising in his stirrups, flung his head full at the fugitive's back. With a squeal of fright the schoolmaster rolled into a mass of weeds by the wayside, and for some minutes he remained there, knowing and remembering nothing.

Next morning farmer Van Tassell's horse was found grazing in a field near Sleepy Hollow, and a man who lived some miles southward reported that he had seen Mr. Crane striding as rapidly along the road to New York as his lean legs could take him, and wearing a pale and serious face as he kept his march. There were yellow stains on the back of his coat, and the man who restored the horse found a smashed pumpkin in the broken bushes beside the road. Ichabod never returned to Tarrytown, and

when Brom Bones, a stout young ploughman and tap-
haunter, married Katrina, people made bold to say
that he knew more about the galloping Hessian than
any one else, though they believed that he never had
reason to be jealous of Ichabod Crane.

STORM SHIP OF THE HUDSON

IT was noised about New Amsterdam, two hundred years ago, that a round and bulky ship
flying Dutch colors from her lofty quarter was
careering up the harbor in the teeth of a north
wind, through the swift waters of an ebbing tide,
and making for the Hudson. A signal from the
Battery to heave to and account for herself being
disregarded, a cannon was trained upon her, and a
ball went whistling through her cloudy and impon-
derable mass, for timbers she had none. Some of
the sailor-folk talked of mirages that rose into the
air of northern coasts and seas, but the wise ones
put their fingers beside their noses and called to
memory the Flying Dutchman, that wanderer of the
seas whose captain, having sworn that he would
round Cape Horn in spite of heaven and hell, has
been beating to and fro along the bleak Fuegian
coast and elsewhere for centuries, being allowed to
land but once in seven years, when he can break the
curse if he finds a girl who will love him. Perhaps Captain Vanderdecken found this maiden of his
hopes in some Dutch settlement on the Hudson, or

perhaps he expiated his rashness by prayer and penitence; howbeit, he never came down again, unless he slipped away to sea in snow or fog so dense that watchers and boatmen saw nothing of his passing. A few old settlers declared the vessel to be the Half Moon, and there were some who testified to seeing that identical ship with Hudson and his spectre crew on board making for the Catskills to hold carouse.

This fleeting vision has been confounded with the storm ship that lurks about the foot of the Palisades and Point-no-Point, cruising through Tappan Zee at night when a gale is coming up. The Hudson is four miles wide at Tappan, and squalls have space enough to gather force; hence, when old skippers saw the misty form of a ship steal out from the shadows of the western hills, then fly like a gull from shore to shore, catching the moonlight on her topsails, but showing no lanterns, they made to windward and dropped anchor, unless their craft were stanch and their pilot's brains unvexed with liquor. On summer nights, when falls that curious silence which is ominous of tempest, the storm ship is not only seen spinning across the mirror surface of the river, but the voices of the crew are heard as they chant at the braces and halyards in words devoid of meaning to the listeners.

The Hudson and its Hills

WHY SPUYTEN DUYVIL IS SO NAMED

THE tide-water creek that forms the upper boundary of Manhattan Island is known to dwellers in tenements round about as "Spittin' Divvle." The proper name of it is Spuyten Duyvil, and this, in turn, is the compression of a celebrated boast by Anthony Van Corlaer. This redoubtable gentleman, famous for fat, long wind, and long whiskers, was trumpeter for the garrison at New Amsterdam, which his countrymen had just bought for twenty-four dollars, and he sounded the brass so sturdily that in the fight between the Dutch and Indians at the Dey Street peach orchard his blasts struck more terror into the red men's hearts than did the matchlocks of his comrades. William the Testy vowed that Anthony and his trumpet were garrison enough for all Manhattan Island, for he argued that no regiment of Yankees would approach near enough to be struck with lasting deafness, as must have happened if they came when Anthony was awake.

Peter Stuyvesant—Peter the Headstrong—showed his appreciation of Anthony's worth by making him his esquire, and when he got news of an English expedition on its way to seize his unoffending colony, he at once ordered Anthony to rouse the villages along the Hudson with a trumpet call to war. The esquire took a hurried leave of six or eight ladies, each of whom delighted to believe that his affections were lavished on her alone, and bravely started northward, his trumpet hanging on one side, a stone bottle, much heavier, depending from the other. It was a stormy evening when he arrived at the upper end of the island, and there was no ferryman in sight, so, after fuming up and down the shore, he swallowed a mighty draught of Dutch courage,—for he was as accomplished a performer on the horn as on the trumpet,—and swore with ornate and voluminous oaths that he would swim the stream "in spite of the devil" [En spuyt den Duyvil].

He plunged in, and had gone half-way across when the Evil One, not to be spited, appeared as a huge moss-bunker, vomiting boiling water and lashing a fiery tail. This dreadful fish seized Anthony by the leg; but the trumpeter was game, for, raising his instrument to his lips, he exhaled his last breath through it in a defiant blast that rang through the woods for miles and made the devil himself let go for a moment. Then he was dragged below, his nose shining through the water more and more faintly, until, at last, all sight of him was lost. The failure of his mission resulted in the downfall of the Dutch in America, for, soon after, the English won a bloodless victory, and St. George's cross flaunted from the ramparts where Anthony had so often saluted the setting sun. But it was years, even then, before he was hushed, for in stormy weather it was claimed that the shrill of his trumpet could be heard near the creek that he had named, sounding above the deeper roar of the blast.

The Hudson and its Hills

THE RAMAPO SALAMANDER

A CURIOUS tale of the Rosicrucians runs to the effect that more than two centuries ago a band of German colonists entered the Ramapo valley and put up houses of stone, like those they had left in the Hartz Mountains, and when the Indians saw how they made knives and other wonderful things out of metal, which they extracted from the rocks by fire, they believed them to be manitous and went away, not wishing to resist their possession of the land. There was treasure here, for High Tor, or Torn Mountain, had been the home of Amasis, youngest of the magi who had followed the star of Bethlehem. He had found his way, through Asia and Alaska, to this country, had taken to wife a native woman, by whom he had a child, and here on the summit he had built a temple. Having refused the sun worship, when the Indians demanded that he should take their faith, he was set upon, and would have been killed had not an earthquake torn the ground at his feet, opening a new channel for the Hudson and precipitating into it every one but the magus and his daughter. To him had been revealed in magic vision the secrets of wealth in the rocks.

The leader in the German colony, one Hugo, was a man of noble origin, who had a wife and two children: a boy, named after himself; a girl,—Mary. Though it had been the custom in the other country to let out the forge fires once in seven years, Hugo

53

opposed that practice in the forge he had built as needless. But his men murmured and talked of the salamander that once in seven years attains its growth in unquenched flame and goes forth doing mischief. On the day when that period was ended the master entered his works and saw the men gazing into the furnace at a pale form that seemed made from flame, that was nodding and turning in the fire, occasionally darting its tongue at them or allowing its tail to fall out and lie along the stone floor. As he came to the door he, too, was transfixed, and the fire seemed burning his vitals, until he felt water sprinkled on his face, and saw that his wife, whom he had left at home too ill to move, stood behind him and was casting holy water into the furnace, speaking an incantation as she did so. At that moment a storm arose, and a rain fell that put out the fire; but as the last glow faded the lady fell dead.

When her children were to be consecrated, seven years later, those who stood outside of the church during the ceremony saw a vivid flash, and the nurse turned from the boy in her fright. She took her hands from her eyes. The child was gone. Twice seven years had passed and the daughter remained unspotted by the world, for, on the night when her father had led her to the top of High Torn Mountain and shown her what Amasis had seen,—the earth spirits in their caves heaping jewels and offering to give them if Hugo would speak the word that binds the free to the earth forces and bars his future for a thousand years,—it was her prayer that brought him to his senses and made the scene below grow dim, though the baleful light of the salamander clinging to the rocks at the bottom of the cave sent a glow into the sky.

Many nights after that the glow was seen on the height and Hugo was missing from his home, but for lack of a pure soul to stand as interpreter he failed to read the words that burned in the triangle on the salamander's back, and returned in rage and jealousy. A knightly man had of late appeared in the settlement, and between him and Mary a tender feeling had arisen, that, however, was unexpressed until, after saving her from the attack of a panther, he had allowed her to fall into his arms. She would willingly then have declared her love for him, but he placed her gently and regretfully from him and said, "When you slept I came to you and put a crown of gems on your head: that was because I was in the power of the earth spirit. Then I had power only over the element of fire, that either consumes or hardens to stone; but now water and life are mine. Behold! Wear these, for thou art worthy." And touching the tears that had fallen from her eyes, they turned into lilies in his hands, and he put them on her brow.

"Shall we meet again?" asked the girl.

"I do not know," said he. "I tread the darkness of the universe alone, and I peril my redemption by yielding to this love of earth. Thou art redeemed already, but I must make my way back to

Myths and Legends

God through obedience tested in trial. Know that
I am one of those that left heaven for love of man.
We were of that subtle element which is flame,—
burning and glowing with love,—and when thy
mother came to me with the power of purity to
cast me out of the furnace, I lost my shape of fire
and took that of a human being,—a child. I have
been with thee often, and was rushing to annihila-
tion, because I could not withstand the ordeal of the
senses. Had I yielded, or found thee other than
thou art, I should have become again an earth spirit.
I have been led away by wish for power, such as I
have in my grasp, and forgot the mission to the suffering. I became a wanderer over the earth until I
reached this land, the land that you call new. Here
was to be my last trial and here I am to pass the gate
of fire."

As he spoke voices arose from the settlement.
" They are coming," said he. The stout form of
Hugo was in advance. With a fierce oath he sprang
on the young man. " He has ruined my household," he cried. " Fling him into the furnace!"
The young man stood waiting, but his brow was
serene. He was seized, and in a few moments had
disappeared through the mouth of the burning pit.
But Mary, looking up, saw a shape in robes of sil-
very light, and it drifted upward until it vanished in
the darkness. The look of horror on her face died
away, and a peace came to it that endured until the
end.

The Hudson and its Hills

CHIEF CROTON

BETWEEN the island of Manhattoes and the Catskills the Hudson shores were plagued with spooks, and even as late as the nineteenth century Hans Anderson, a man who tilled a farm back of Peekskill, was worried into his grave by the leaden-face likeness of a British spy whom he had hanged on General Putnam's orders. "Old Put" doubtless enjoyed immunity from this vexatious creature, because he was born with few nerves. A region especially afflicted was the confluence of the Croton and the Hudson, for the Kitchawan burying-ground was here, and the red people being disturbed by the tramping of white men over their graves, "the walking sachems of Teller's Point" were nightly to be met on their errands of protest.

These Indians had built a palisade on Croton Point, and here they made their last stand against their enemies from the north. Throughout the fight old chief Croton stood on the wall with arrows showering around him, and directed the resistance with the utmost calm. Not until every one of his men was dead and the fort was going up in flame about him did he confess defeat. Then standing amid the charring timbers, he used his last breath in calling down the curse of the Great Spirit against the foe. As the victorious enemy rushed into the enclosure to secure the scalps of the dead he fell lifeless into the fire, and their jubilant yell was lost upon his ears. Yet, he could not rest nor bear to leave his ancient home, even after death, and often his form, in musing attitude, was seen moving through the woods. When a manor was built on the ruins of his fort, he appeared to the master of it, to urge him into the Continental army, and having seen this behest obeyed and laid a solemn injointure to keep the freedom of the land forever, he vanished, and never appeared again.

THE RETREAT FROM MAHOPAC

AFTER the English had secured the city of New Amsterdam and had begun to extend their settlements along the Hudson, the Indians congregated in large numbers about Lake Mahopac, and rejected all overtures for the purchase of that region. In their resolution they were sustained by their young chief Omoyao, who refused to abandon on any terms the country where his fathers had so long hunted, fished, and built their lodges. A half-breed, one Joliper, a member of this tribe, was secretly in the pay of the English, but the allurements and insinuations that he put forth on their behalf were as futile as the breathing of wind in the leaves. At last the white men grew angry. Have the land they would, by evil course if good ways were refused, and commissioning Joliper to act for them in a decisive manner, they guaranteed to supply him with forces if his negotiations fell through. This man never thought it needful to negotiate. He knew the temper of his tribe and he was too jealous of his chief to go to him for favors, because he loved Maya, the chosen one of Omoyao.

At the door of Maya's tent he entreated her to go with him to the white settlements, and on her refusal he broke into angry threats, declaring, in the self-forgetfulness of passion, that he would kill her lover and lead the English against the tribe. Unknown to both Omoyao had overheard this interview, and he immediately sent runners to tell all warriors of his people to meet him at once on the island in the lake. Though the runners were cautioned to keep their errand secret, it is probable that Joliper suspected that the alarm had gone forth, and he resolved to strike at once; so he summoned his renegades, stole into camp next evening and made toward Maya's wigwam, intending to take her to a place of safety. Seeing the chief at the door, he shot an arrow at him, but the shaft went wide and slew the girl's father. Realizing, upon this assault, that he was outwitted and that his people were outnumbered, the chief called to Maya to meet him at the island, and plunged into the brush, after seeing that she had taken flight in an opposite direction. The vengeful Joliper was close behind him with his renegades, and the chief was captured; then, that he might not communicate with his people or delay the operations against them, it was resolved to put him to death.

Myths and Legends

He was tied to a tree, the surrounding wood was set on fire, and he was abandoned to his fate, his enemies leaving him to destruction in their haste to reach the place of the council and slay or capture all who were there. Hardly were they out of hearing ere the plash of a paddle sounded through the roar of flame and Maya sprang upon the bank, cut her lover's bonds, and with him made toward the island, which they reached by a protected way before the assailants had arrived. They told the story of Joliper's cruelty and treason, and when his boats were seen coming in to shore they had eyes and hands only for Joliper. He was the first to land. Hardly had he touched the strand before he was surrounded by a frenzied crowd and had fallen bleeding from a hundred gashes.

The Indians were overpowered after a brief and bloody resistance. They took safety in flight. Omoyao and Maya, climbing upon the rock above their " council chamber," found that while most of their people had escaped their own retreat was cut off, and that it would be impossible to reach any of the canoes. They preferred death to torture and captivity, so, hand in hand, they leaped together down the cliff, and the English claimed the land next day.

The Hudson and its Hills

NIAGARA

THE cataract of Niagara (properly pronounced
Nee-ah-gah-rah), or Oniahgarah, is as fatal as
it is fascinating, beautiful, sublime, and the casualties
occurring there justify the tradition that "the Thun-
dering Water asks two victims every year." It was
reputed, before white men looked for the first time
on these falls—and what thumping yarns they told
about them!—that two lives were lost here annually,
and this average has been kept up by men and women
who fall into the flood through accident, recklessness
or despair, while bloody battles have been fought on
the shores, and vessels have been hurled over the
brink, to be dashed to splinters on the rocks.

The sound of the cataract was declared to be the
voice of a mighty spirit that dwelt in the waters,
and in former centuries the Indians offered to it a
yearly sacrifice. This sacrifice was a maiden of the
tribe, who was sent over in a white canoe, decorated
with fruit and flowers, and the girls contended for
this honor, for the brides of Manitou were objects
of a special grace in the happy hunting-grounds.
The last recorded sacrifice was in 1679, when Lela-
wala, the daughter of chief Eagle Eye, was chosen,
in spite of the urgings and protests of the chevalier
La Salle, who had been trying to restrain the people
from their idolatries by an exposition of the Christian dogma. To his protests he received the unexpected answer, "Your words witness against you.

Myths and Legends

Christ, you say, set us an example. We will follow
it. Why should one death be great, while our sacrifice is horrible ?" So the tribe gathered at the bank
to watch the sailing of the white canoe. The chief
watched the embarkation with the stoicism usual to
the Indian when he is observed by others, but when
the little bark swung out into the current his affection
mastered him, and he leaped into his own canoe and
tried to overtake his daughter. In a moment both
were beyond the power of rescue. After their death
they were changed into spirits of pure strength and
goodness, and live in a crystal heaven so far beneath
the fall that its roaring is a music to them : she, the
maid of the mist ; he, the ruler of the cataract. Another version of the legend makes a lover and his
mistress the chief actors. Some years later a patri-
arch of the tribe and all his sons went over the fall
when the white men had seized their lands, preferring
death to flight or war.

In about the year 200 the Stone Giants waded
across the river below the falls on their northward
march. These beings were descended from an ancient family, and being separated from their stock in
the year 150 by the breaking of a vine bridge across
the Mississippi, they left that region. Indian Pass,
in the Adirondacks, bore the names of Otneyarheh,
Stony Giants ; Ganosgwah, Giants Clothed in Stone ;
and Dayohjegago, Place Where the Storm Clouds
Fight the Great Serpent. Giants and serpents were
held to be harmful inventions of the Evil Spirit, and

the Lightning god, catching up clouds as he stood on
the crags, broke them open, tore their lightnings out
and hurled them against the monsters. These cannibals had almost exterminated the Iroquois, for they
were of immense size and had made themselves almost invincible by rolling daily in the sand until
their flesh was like stone. The Holder of the
Heavens, viewing their evil actions from on high,
came down disguised as one of their number—he
used often to meditate on Manitou Rock, at the
Whirlpool—and leading them to a valley near
Onondaga, on pretence of guiding them to a fairer
country, he stood on a hill above them and hurled
rocks upon their heads until all, save one, who fled
into the north, were dead. Yet, in the fulness of
time, new children of the Stone Giants (mail-clad
Europeans?) entered the region again and were destroyed by the Great Spirit,—oddly enough where
the famous fraud known as the Cardiff giant was alleged to have been found. The Onondagas believed
this statue to be one of their ancient foes.

THE DEFORMED OF ZOAR

THE valley of Zoar, in western New York, is so
surrounded by hills that its discoverers—a religious people, who gave it a name from Scripture—
said, " This is Zoar; it is impregnable. From her
we will never go." And truly, for lack of roads, they
found it so hard to get out, having got in, that they

did not leave it. Among the early settlers here were
people of a family named Wright, whose house became a sort of inn for the infrequent traveller, inasmuch as they were not troubled with piety, and had
no scruples against the selling of drink and the playing of cards at late hours. A peddler passed through
the valley on his way to Buffalo and stopped at the
Wright house for a lodging, but before he went to
bed he incautiously showed a number of golden
trinkets from his pack and drew a considerable
quantity of money out of his pocket when he paid
the fee for his lodging. Hardly had he fallen asleep
before his greedy hosts were in the room, searching
for his money. Their lack of caution caused him to
awake, and as he found them rifling his pockets and
his pack he sprang up and showed fight.

A blow sent him to the bottom of the stairs, where
his attempt to escape was intercepted, and the family
closed around him and bound his arms and legs.
They showed him the money they had taken and
asked where he had concealed the rest. He vowed
that it was all he had. They insisted that he had
more, and seizing a knife from the table the elder
Wright slashed off one of his toes "to make him
confess." No result came from this, and six toes
were cut off,—three from each foot; then, in disgust, the unhappy peddler was knocked on the head
and flung through a trap-door into a shallow cellar.
Presently he arose and tried to draw himself out, but
with hatchet and knife they chopped away his fin-

gers and he fell back. Even the women shared in
this work, and leaned forward to gaze into the cellar
to see if he might yet be dead. While listening,
they heard the man invoke the curse of heaven on
them : he asked that they should wear the mark of
crime even to the fourth generation, by coming into
the world deformed and mutilated as he was then.
And it was so. The next child born in that house
had round, hoof-like feet, with only two toes, and
hands that tapered from the wrist into a single long
finger. And in time there were twenty people so
deformed in the valley : " the crab-clawed Zoarites"
they were called.

HORSEHEADS

THE feeling recently created by an attempt to
fasten the stupid names of Fairport or of
North Elmira on the village in central New York
that, off and on for fifty years, had been called Horseheads, caused an inquiry as to how that singular
name chanced to be adopted for a settlement. In
1779, when General Sullivan was retiring toward
the base of his supplies after a destructive campaign
against the Indians in Genesee County, he stopped
near this place and rested his troops. The country
was then rude, unbroken, and still beset with
enemies, however, and when the march was resumed
it was thought best to gain time over a part of the
way by descending the Chemung River on rafts.

Myths and Legends

As there were no appliances for building large floats, and the depth of the water was not known, the general ordered a destruction of all impedimenta that could be got rid of, and commanded that the poor and superfluous horses should be killed. His order was obeyed. As soon as the troops had gone, the wolves, that were then abundant, came forth and devoured the carcasses of the steeds, so that the clean-picked bones were strewn widely over the camp-ground. When the Indians ventured back into this region, some of them piled the skulls of the horses into heaps, and these curious monuments were found by white settlers who came into the valley some years later, and who named their village Horseheads, in commemoration of these relics. The Indians were especially loth to leave this region, for their tradition was that it had been the land of the Senecas from immemorial time, the tribe being descended from a couple that had a home on a hill near Horseheads.

KAYUTA AND WANETA

THE Indians loved our lakes. They had eyes for their beauty, and to them they were abodes of gracious spirits. They used to say of Oneida Lake, that when the Great Spirit formed the world "his smile rested on its waters and Frenchman's Island rose to greet it; he laughed and Lotus Island came up to listen." So they built lodges on their shores and skimmed their waters in canoes. Much of their history relates to them, and this is a tale of the Senecas that was revived a few years ago by the discovery of a deer-skin near Lakes Waneta and Keuka, New York, on which some facts of the history were rudely drawn, for all Indians are artists.

Waneta, daughter of a chief, had plighted her troth to Kayuta, a hunter of a neighboring tribe with which her people were at war. Their tryst was held at twilight on the farther shore of the lake from her village, and it was her gayety and happiness, after these meetings had taken place, that roused the suspicion and jealousy of Weutha, who had marked her for his bride against the time when he should have won her father's consent by some act of bravery. Shadowing the girl as she stole into the forest one evening, he saw her enter her canoe and row to a densely wooded spot; he heard a call like the note of a quail, then an answer; then Kayuta emerged on the shore, lifted the maiden from her little bark, and the twain sat down beside the water to listen to the lap of its waves and watch the stars come out.

Hurrying back to camp, the spy reported that an enemy was near them, and although Waneta had regained her wigwam by another route before the company of warriors had reached the lake, Kayuta was seen, pursued, and only escaped with difficulty. Next evening, not knowing what had happened after her homeward departure on the previous night

Myths and Legends

—for the braves deemed it best to keep the knowledge of their military operations from the women —the girl crept away to the lake again and rowed to the accustomed place, but while waiting for the quail call a twig dropped on the water beside her. With a quick instinct that civilization has spoiled she realized this to be a warning, and remaining perfectly still, she allowed her boat to drift toward shore, presently discovering that her lover was standing waist-deep in the water. In a whisper he told her that they were watched, and bade her row to a dead pine that towered at the foot of the lake, where he would soon meet her. At that instant an arrow grazed his side and flew quivering into the canoe.

Pushing the boat on its course and telling her to hasten, Kayuta sprang ashore, sounded the war-whoop, and as Weutha rose into sight he clove his skull with a tomahawk. Two other braves now leaped forward, but, after a struggle, Kayuta left them dead or senseless, too. He would have stayed to tear their scalps off had he not heard his name uttered in a shriek of agony from the end of the lake, and, tired and bleeding though he was, he bounded along its margin like a deer, for the voice that he heard was Waneta's. He reached the blasted pine, gave one look, and sank to the earth. Presently other Indians came, who had heard the noise of fighting, and burst upon him with yells and brandished weapons, but something in his look restrained them from a close advance. His eyes were fixed on a string of beads that lay on the bottom of the lake, just off shore, and when the meaning of it came to them, the savages thought no more of killing, but moaned their grief; for Waneta, in stepping from her canoe to wade ashore, had been caught and swallowed by a quagmire. All night and all next day Kayuta sat there like a man of stone. Then, just as the hour fell when he was used to meet his love, his heart broke, and he joined her in the spirit land.

THE DROP STAR

A LITTLE maid of three years was missing from her home on the Genesee. She had gone to gather water-lilies and did not return. Her mother, almost crazed with grief, searched for days, weeks, months, before she could resign herself to the thought that her little one—Kayutah, the Drop Star, the Indians called her—had indeed been drowned. Years went by. The woman's home was secure against pillage, for it was no longer the one house of a white family in that region, and the Indians had retired farther and farther into the wilderness. One day a hunter came to the woman and said, "I have seen old Skenandoh,—the last of his tribe, thank God!— who bade me say this to you: that the ice is broken, and he knows of a hill of snow where a red berry grows that shall be yours if you will claim it." When the meaning of this message came upon her the woman fainted, but on recovering speech she despatched her nephew to the hut of the aged chief and passed that night in prayer.

The young man set off at sunset, and by hard riding, over dim trails, with only stars for light, he came in the gray of dawn to an upright timber, colored red and hung with scalps, that had been cut from white men's heads at the massacre of Wyoming. The place they still call Painted Post. Without drawing rein he sped along the hills that hem Lake Seneca, then, striking deeper into the wilds, he reached a smaller lake, and almost fell from his saddle before a rude tent near the shore. A new grave had been dug close by, and he shuddered to think that perhaps he had come too late, but a wrinkled Indian stepped forth at that moment and waited his word.

"I come," cried the youth, "to see the berry that springs from snow."

"You come in time," answered Skenandoh. "No, 'tis not in that grave. It is my own child that is buried there. She was as a sister to the one you seek, and she bade me restore the Drop Star to her mother,—the squaw that we know as the New Moon's Light."

Stepping into the wigwam, he emerged again, clasping the wrist of a girl of eighteen, whose robe he tore asunder at the throat, showing the white breast, and on it a red birth-mark; then, leading her to the young man, he said, "And now I must go to the setting sun." He slung a pouch about him, loaded, not with arms and food, but stones, stepped into his canoe, and paddled out upon the water, singing as he went a melancholy chant—his death-song. On gaining the middle of the lake he swung his tomahawk and clove the bottom of the frail boat, so that it filled in a moment and the chief sank from sight. The young man took his cousin to her over-joyed mother, helped to win her back to the ways of civilized life, and eventually married her. She took her Christian name again, but left to the lake on whose banks she had lived so long her Indian name of Drop Star—Kayutah.

THE PROPHET OF PALMYRA

IT was at Palmyra, New York, that the principles of Mormonism were first enunciated by Joseph Smith, who claimed to have found the golden plates of the Book of Mormon in a hill-side in neighboring Manchester,—the " Hill of Cumorah,"—to which he was led by angels. The plates were written in characters similar to the masonic cabala, and he translated them by divine aid, giving to the world the result of his discovery. The Hebrew prophet Mormon was the alleged author of the record, and his son Moroni buried it. The basis of Mormon-ism was, however, an unpublished novel, called " The Manuscript Found," that was read to Sidney Rigdon (afterwards a Mormon elder) by its author, a clergyman, and that formulated a creed for a hypothetical church. Smith had a slight local celebrity, for he and his father were operators with the divining-rod, and when he appropriated this creed— a harmless and beneficent one, for polygamy was a later " inspiration" of Brigham Young—and began to preach it, in 1844, it gained many converts. His arrogation of the presidency of the " Church of Latter Day Saints" and other rash performances won for him the enmity of the Gentiles, who imprisoned and killed him at Carthage, Missouri, leaving Brigham Young to lead the people across the deserts to Salt Lake, where they prospered through thrift and industry.

It was claimed that in the van of this army, on the march to Utah, was often seen a venerable man with silver beard, who never spoke, but who would point the way whenever the pilgrims were faint or discouraged. When they reached the spot where the temple was afterwards built, he struck his staff into the earth and vanished.

At Hydesville, near Palmyra, spiritualism, as it is commonly called, came into being on March 31, 1849, when certain of the departed announced themselves by thumping on doors and tables in the house of the Fox family, the survivors of which confessed the fraud nearly forty years after. It is of interest to note that the ground whence these new religions sprang was peopled by the Onondagas, the sacerdotal class of the Algonquin tribe, who have preserved the ancient religious rites of that great family until this day.

The Hudson and its Hills

A VILLAIN'S CREMATION

BRAMLEY'S Mountain, near the present village of Bloomfield, New York, on the edge of the Catskill group, was the home of a young couple that had married with rejoicing and had taken up the duties and pleasures of housekeeping with enthusiasm. To be sure, in those days housekeeping was not a thing to be much afraid of, and the servant question had not come up for discussion. The housewives did the work themselves, and the husband had no valets. The domicile of this particular pair was merely a tent of skins stretched around a frame of poles, and their furniture consisted principally of furs strewn over the earth floor; but they loved each other truly. The girl was thankful to be taken from her home to live, because, up to the time of her marriage, she had been persecuted by a morose and ill-looking fellow of her tribe, who laid siege to her affection with such vehemence that the more he pleaded the greater was her dislike; and now she hoped that she had seen the last of him. But that was not to be. He lurked about the wigwam of the pair, torturing himself with the sight of their felicity, and awaiting his chance to prove his hate.

This chance came when the husband had gone to Lake Delaware to fish, for he rowed after and gave battle in the middle of the pond. Taken by surprise, and being insufficiently armed, the husband was killed and his body flung into the water. Then, casting an affectionate leer at the wife who had watched this act of treachery and malice with speechless horror from the mountain-side, he drove his canoe ashore and set off in pursuit of her. She retreated so slowly as to allow him to keep her in sight, and when she entered a cave he pressed forward eagerly, believing that now her escape was impossible ; but she had purposely trapped him there, for she had already explored a tortuous passage that led to the upper air, and by this she had left the cavern in safety while he was groping and calling in the dark. Returning to the entrance, she loosened, by a jar, a ledge that overhung it, so that the door was almost blocked ; then, gathering light wood from the dry trees around her, she made a fire and hurled the burning sticks into the prison where the wretch was howling, until he was dead in smoke and flame. When his yells and curses had been silenced she told a friend what she had done, then going back to the lake, she sang her death-song and cast herself into the water, hoping thus to rejoin her husband.

THE MONSTER MOSQUITO

THEY have some pretty big mosquitoes in New Jersey and on Long Island, but, if report of their ancestry is true, they have degenerated in size and voracity ; for the grandfather of all mosquitoes used to live in the neighborhood of Fort Onondaga,

The Hudson and its Hills

New York, and sallying out whenever he was hungry, would eat an Indian or two and pick his teeth with their ribs. The red men had no arms that could prevail against it, but at last the Holder of the Heavens, hearing their cry for aid, came down and attacked the insect. Finding that it had met its match, the mosquito flew away so rapidly that its assailant could hardly keep it in sight. It flew around the great lake, then turned eastward again. It sought help vainly of the witches that brooded in the sink-holes, or Green Lakes (near Janesville, New York), and had reached the salt lake of Onondaga when its pursuer came up and killed it, the creature piling the sand into hills in its dying struggles.

As its blood poured upon the earth it became small mosquitoes, that gathered about the Holder of the Heavens and stung him so sorely that he half repented the service that he had done to men. The Tuscaroras say that this was one of two monsters that stood on opposite banks of the Seneca River and slew all men that passed. Hiawatha killed the other one. On their reservation is a stone, marked by the form of the Sky Holder, that shows where he rested during the chase, while his tracks were until lately seen south of Syracuse, alternating with footprints of the mosquito, which were shaped like those of a bird, and twenty inches long. At Brighton, New York, where these marks appeared, they were reverentially renewed by the Indians for many years.

Myths and Legends

THE GREEN PICTURE

IN a cellar in Green Street, Schenectady, there appeared, some years ago, the silhouette of a human form, painted on the floor in mould. It was swept and scrubbed away, but presently it was there again, and month by month, after each removal, it returned: a mass of fluffy mould, always in the shape of a recumbent man. When it was found that the house stood on the site of the old Dutch burial ground, the gossips fitted this and that together and concluded that the mould was planted by a spirit whose mortal part was put to rest a century and more ago, on the spot covered by the house, and that the spirit took this way of apprising people that they were trespassing on its grave. Others held that foul play had been done, and that a corpse, hastily and shallowly buried, was yielding itself back to the damp cellar in vegetable form, before its resolution into simpler elements. But a darker meaning was that it was the outline of a vampire that vainly strove to leave its grave, and could not because a virtuous spell had been worked about the place.

A vampire is a dead man who walks about seeking for those whose blood he can suck, for only by supplying new life to its cold limbs can he keep the privilege of moving about the earth. He fights his way from his coffin, and those who meet his gray and stiffened shape, with fishy eyes and blackened mouth, lurking by open windows, biding his time to

The Hudson and its Hills

steal in and drink up a human life, fly from him in
terror and disgust. In northern Rhode Island those
who die of consumption are believed to be victims
of vampires who work by charm, draining the blood
by slow draughts as they lie in their graves. To
lay this monster he must be taken up and burned;
at least, his heart must be; and he must be disin-
terred in the daytime when he is asleep and un-
aware. If he died with blood in his heart he has
this power of nightly resurrection. As late as 1892
the ceremony of heart-burning was performed at
Exeter, Rhode Island, to save the family of a dead
woman that was threatened with the same disease
that removed her, namely, consumption. But the
Schenectady vampire has yielded up all his sub-
stance, and the green picture is no more.

THE NUNS OF CARTHAGE

A T Carthage, New York, where the Black River
bends gracefully about a point, there was a
stanch old house, built in the colonial fashion and
designed for the occupancy of some family of hospitality and wealth, but the family died out or moved
away, and for some years it remained deserted. During
the war of 1812 the village gossips were excited by
the appearance of carpenters, painters and uphol-
sterers, and it was evident that the place was to be
restored to its manorial dignities; but their curiosity
was deepened instead of satisfied when, after the

77

house had been put in order and high walls built around it, the occupants presented themselves as four young women in the garb of nuns. Were they daughters of the family ? Were they English sympathizers in disguise, seeking asylum in the days of trouble ? Had they registered a vow of celibacy until their lovers should return from the war ? Were they on a secret and diplomatic errand ? None ever knew, at least in Carthage. The nuns lived in great privacy, but in a luxury before unequalled in that part of the country. They kept a gardener, they received from New York wines and delicacies that others could not afford, and when they took the air, still veiled, it was behind a splendid pair of bays.

One afternoon, just after the close of the war, a couple of young American officers went to the convent, and, contrary to all precedent, were admitted. They remained within all that day, and no one saw them leave, but a sound of wheels passed through the street that evening. Next day there were no signs of life about the place, nor the day following, nor the next. The savage dog was quiet and the garden walks had gone unswept. Some neighbors climbed over the wall and reported that the place had been deserted. Why and by whom no one ever knew, but a cloud remained upon its title until a recent day, for it was thought that at some time the nuns might return.

The Hudson and its Hills

THE SKULL IN THE WALL

A SKULL is built into the wall above the door of the court-house at Goshen, New York. It was taken from a coffin unearthed in 1842, when the foundation of the building was laid. People said there was no doubt about it, only Claudius Smith could have worn that skull, and he deserved to be publicly pilloried in that manner. Before the Revolutionary war Smith was a farmer in Monroe, New York, and being prosperous enough to feel the king's taxes no burden, to say nothing of his jealousy of the advantage that an independent government would be to the hopes of his poorer neighbors, he declared for the king. After the declaration of independence had been published, his sympathies were illustrated in an unpleasantly practical manner by gathering a troop of other Tories about him, and, emboldened by the absence of most of the men of his vicinage in the colonial army, he began to harass the country as grievously in foray as the red-coats were doing in open field.

He pillaged houses and barns, then burned them; he insulted women, he drove away cattle and horses, he killed several persons who had undertaken to defend their property. His "campaigns" were managed with such secrecy that nobody knew when or whence to look for him. His murder of Major Nathaniel Strong, of Blooming Grove, roused indignation to such a point that a united effort was made to catch him, a money reward for success acting as a stimulus to the vigilance of the hunters, and at last he was captured on Long Island. He was sent back to Goshen, tried, convicted, and on January 22, 1779, was hanged, with five of his band. The bodies of the culprits were buried in the jail-yard, on the spot where the court-house stands, and old residents identified Smith's skeleton, when it was accidentally exhumed, by its uncommon size. A farmer from an adjacent town made off with a thigh bone, and a mason clapped mortar into the empty skull and cemented it into the wall, where it long remained.

THE HAUNTED MILL

AMONG the settlers in the Adirondacks, forty or fifty years ago, was Henry Clymer, from Brooklyn, who went up to Little Black Creek and tried to make a farm out of the gnarly, stumpy land; but being a green hand at that sort of thing, he soon gave it up and put up the place near Northwood, that is locally referred to as the haunted mill. When the first slab was cut, a big party was on hand to cheer and eat pie in honor of the Clymers, for Mr. Clymer, who was a dark, hearty, handsome fellow, and his bright young wife had been liberal in their hospitality. The couple had made some talk, they were so loving before folks—too loving to last; and, besides, it was evident that Mrs. Clymer was used to a better station in life than her husband. It was while the crowd was laughing and chattering at the picnic-table of new boards from the mill that Mrs. Clymer stole away to her modest little house, and a neighbor who had followed her was an accidental witness to a singular episode. Mrs. Clymer was kneeling beside her bed, crying over the picture of a child, when Clymer entered unexpectedly and attempted to take the picture from her.

She faced him defiantly. " You kept that because it looked like him, I reckon," he said. " You might run back to him. You know what he'd call you and where you'd stand with your aristocracy."

The woman pointed to the door, and the man left without another word, and so did the listener. Next morning the body of Mrs. Clymer was found hanging to a beam in the mill. At the inquest the husband owned that he had " had a few words" with her on the previous day, and thought that she must have suddenly become insane. The jury took this view. News of the suicide was printed in some of the city papers, and soon after that the gossips had another sensation, for a fair-haired man, also from Brooklyn, arrived at the place and asked where the woman was buried. When he found the grave he sat beside it for some time, his head resting on his hand ; then he inquired for Clymer, but Clymer, deadly pale, had gone into the woods as soon as he heard that a stranger had arrived. The new-comer went to Trenton, where he ordered a gravestone bearing the single word " Estella" to be placed

where the woman's body had been interred. Clymer
quickly sold out and disappeared. The mill never
prospered, and has long been in a ruinous condition.
People of the neighborhood think that the ghost of
Mrs. Clymer—was that her name ?—still troubles it,
and they pass the place with quickened steps.

OLD INDIAN FACE

ON Lower Ausable Pond is a large, ruddy rock
showing a huge profile, with another, resem-
bling a pappoose, below it. When the Tahawi ruled
this region their sachem lived here at " the Dark
Cup," as they called this lake, a man renowned for
virtue and remarkable, in his age, for gentleness.
When his children had died and his manly grandson, who was the old man's hope, had followed
them to the land of the cloud mountains, Adota's
heart withered within him, and standing beneath
this rock, he addressed his people, recounting what
he had done for them, how he had swept their
enemies from the Lakes of the Clustered Stars (the
Lower Saranac) and Silver Sky (Upper Saranac)
to the Lake of Wandah, gaining a land where they
might hunt and fish in peace. The little one, the
Star, had been ravished away to crown the brow of
the thunder god, who, even now, was advancing
across the peaks, bending the woods and lighting
the valleys with his jagged torches.

Life was nothing to him longer ; he resigned it.

The Hudson and its Hills

As he spoke these words he fell back, and the breath passed out of him. Then came the thunder god, and with an appalling burst of fire sent the people cowering. The roar that followed seemed to shake the earth, but the medicine-man of the tribe stood still, listening to the speech of the god in the clouds. "Tribe of the Tahawi," he translated, "Adota treads the star-path to the happy hunting-grounds, and the sun is shining on his heart. He will never walk among you again, but the god loves both him and you, and he will set his face on the mountains. Look!" And, raising their eyes, they beheld the likeness of Adota and of his beloved child, the Star, graven by lightning-stroke on the cliff. There they buried the body of Adota and held their solemn festivals until the white men drove them out of the country.

THE DIVISION OF THE SARANACS

IN the middle of the last century a large body of Saranac Indians occupied the forests of the Upper Saranac through which ran the Indian carrying-place, called by them the Eagle Nest Trail. Whenever they raided the Tahawi on the slopes of Mount Tahawus (Sky-splitter), there was a pleasing rivalry between two young athletes, called the Wolf and the Eagle, as to which would carry off the more scalps, and the tribe was divided in admiration of them. There was one who did not share this liking: an old sachem, one of the wizards who had escaped when the Great Spirit locked these workers of evil in the hollow trees that stood beside the trail. In their struggles to escape the less fortunate ones thrust their arms through the closing bark, and they are seen there, as withered trunks and branches, to this day. Oquarah had not been softened by this exhibition of danger nor the qualification of mercy that allowed him still to exist. Rather he was more bitter when he saw, as he fancied, that the tribe thought more of the daring and powerful warriors than it did of the bent and malignant-minded counsellor.

It was in the moon of green leaves that the two young men set off to hunt the moose, and on the next day the Wolf returned alone. He explained that in the hunt they had been separated; he had called for hours for his friend, and had searched so long that he concluded he must have returned ahead of him. But he was not at the camp. Up rose the sachem with visage dark. "I hear a forked tongue," he cried. "The Wolf was jealous of the Eagle and his teeth have cut into his heart."

"The Wolf cannot lie," answered the young man.

"Where is the Eagle?" angrily shouted the sachem, clutching his hatchet.

"The Wolf has said," replied the other.

The old sachem advanced upon him, but as he raised his axe to strike, the wife of the Wolf threw herself before her husband, and the steel sank into her brain. The sachem fell an instant later with the Wolf's knife in his heart, and instantly the camp was in turmoil. Before the day had passed it had been broken up, and the people were divided into factions, for it was no longer possible to hold it together in peace. The Wolf, with half of the people, went down the Sounding River to new hunting-grounds, and the earth that separated the families was reddened whenever one side met the other.

Years had passed when, one morning, the upper tribe saw a canoe advancing across the Lake of the Silver Sky. An old man stepped from it: he was the Eagle. After the Wolf had left him he had fallen into a cleft in a rock, and had lain helpless until found by hunters who were on their way to Canada. He had joined the British against the French, had married a northern squaw, but had returned to die among the people of his early love. Deep was his sorrow that his friend should have been accused of doing him an injury, and that the once happy tribe should have been divided by that allegation. The warriors and sachems of both branches were summoned to a council, and in his presence they swore a peace, so that in the fulness of time he was able to die content. That peace was always kept.

Myths and Legends

AN EVENT IN INDIAN PARK

IT was during the years when the Saranacs were divided that Howling Wind, one of the young men of Indian Carry, saw and fell in love with a girl of the family on Tupper Lake. He quickly found a way to tell his liking, and the couple met often in the woods and on the shore. He made bold to row her around the quieter bays, and one moonlight evening he took her to Devil's Rock, or Devil's Pulpit, where he told her the story of the place. This was to the effect that the fiend had paddled, on timbers, by means of his tail, to that rock, and had assembled fish and game about him in large numbers by telling them that he was going to preach to them, instead of which moral procedure he pounced upon and ate all that were within his grasp.

As so often happened in Indian history, the return of these lovers was seen by a disappointed rival, who had hurried back to camp and secured the aid of half a dozen men to arrest the favored one as soon as he should land. The capture was made after a struggle, and Howling Wind was dragged to the chief's tent for sentence. That sentence was death, and with a refinement of cruelty that was rare even among the Indians, the girl was ordered to execute it. She begged and wept to no avail. An axe was put into her hands, and she was ordered to despatch the prisoner. She took the weapon; her face grew stern and the tears dried on her cheeks; her lover, bound to a tree, gazed at her in amazement; his rival watched, almost in glee. Slowly the girl crossed the open space to her lover. She raised the tomahawk and at a blow severed the thongs that held him, then, like a flash, she leaped upon his rival, who had sprung forward to interfere, and clove his skull with a single stroke. The lovers fled as only those can fly who run for life. Happily for them, they met a party from the Carry coming to rescue Howling Wind from the danger to which his courtship had exposed him, and it was even said that this party entered the village and by presenting knives and arrows at the breast of the chief obtained his now superfluous consent to the union of the fugitives. The pair reached the Carry in safety and lived a long and happy life together.

THE INDIAN PLUME

BRIGHTEST flower that grows beside the brooks is the scarlet blossom of the Indian plume : the blood of Lenawee. Hundreds of years ago she lived happily among her brother and sister Saranacs beside Stony Creek, the Stream of the Snake, and was soon to marry the comely youth who, for the speed of his foot, was called the Arrow. But one summer the Quick Death came on the people, and as the viewless devil stalked through the village young and old fell before him. The Arrow was the first to die. In vain the Prophet smoked the Great Calumet: its smoke ascending took no shape that he could read. In vain was the white dog killed to take aloft the people's sins. But at last the Great Spirit himself came down to the mountain called the Storm Darer, splendid in lightning, awful in his thunder voice and robe of cloud. "My wrath is against you for your sins," he cried, "and naught but human blood will appease it."

In the morning the Prophet told his message, and all sat silent for a time. Then Lenawee entered the circle. "Lenawee is a blighted flower," she sobbed. "Let her blood flow for her people." And catching a knife from the Prophet's belt, she ran with it to the stream on which she and the Arrow had so often floated in their canoe. In another moment her blood had bedewed the earth. "Lay me with the Arrow," she murmured, and, smiling in their sad faces, breathed her last. The demon of the quick death shrank from the spot, and the Great Spirit smiled once more on the tribe that could produce such heroism. Lenawee's body was placed beside her lover's, and next morning, where her blood had spilt, the ground was pure, and on it grew in slender spires a new flower,—the Indian plume: the transformed blood of sacrifice. The people loved that flower in all years after. They decked their hair and dresses with it and made a feast in its honor. When parents taught their children the beauty of unselfishness they used as its emblem a stalk of Indian plume.

The Hudson and its Hills

BIRTH OF THE WATER-LILY

BACK from his war against the Tahawi comes the Sun, chief of the Lower Saranacs,—back to the Lake of the Clustered Stars, afterward called, by dullards, Tupper's Lake. Tall and invincible he comes among his people, boasting of his victories, Indian fashion, and stirring the scalps that hang at his breast. " The Eagle screams," he cries. " He greets the chief, the Blazing Sun. Wayotah has made the Tahawi tremble. They fly from him. Hooh, hooh! He is the chief." Standing apart with wistful glance stands Oseetah, the Bird. She loves the strong young chief, but she knows that another has his promise, and she dares not hope; yet the chief loves her, and when the feasting is over he follows her footprints to the shore, where he sees her canoe turning the point of an island. He silently pursues and comes upon her as she sits waving and moaning. He tries to embrace her, but she draws apart. He asks her to sing to him; she bids him begone.

He takes a more imperious tone and orders her to listen to her chief. She moves away. He darts toward her. Turning on him a face of sorrow, she runs to the edge of a steep rock and waves him back. He hastens after. Then she springs and disappears in the deep water. The Sun plunges after her and swims with mad strength here and there. He calls. There is no answer. Slowly he returns to the village and tells the people what has happened. The Bird's parents are stricken and the Sun moans in his sleep. At noon a hunter comes in with strange tidings: flowers are growing on the water! The people go to their canoes and row to the Island of Elms. There, in a cove, the still water is enamelled with flowers, some as white as snow, filling the air with perfume, others strong and yellow, like the lake at sunset.

"Explain to us," they cry, turning to the old Medicine of his tribe, "for this was not so yesterday." "It is our daughter," he answered. "These flowers are the form she takes. The white is her purity, the yellow her love. You shall see that her heart will close when the sun sets, and will reopen at his coming." And the young chief went apart and bowed his head.

ROGERS'S SLIDE

THE shores of Lakes George and Champlain were ravaged by war. Up and down those lovely waters swept the barges of French and English, and the green hills rang to the shrill of bugles, the boom of cannon, and the yell of savages. Fiction and history have been weft across the woods and the memory of deeds still echoes among the heights. It was at Glen's Falls, in the cave on the rock in the middle of the river, that the brave Uncas held the watch with Hawkeye. Bloody Defile and Bloody Pond,

The Hudson and its Hills

between there and Lake George, take their names from the "Bloody morning scout" sent out by Sir William Johnson on a September day in 1755 to check Dieskau until Fort William Henry could be completed. In the action that ensued, Colonel Williams, founder of Williams College, and Captain Grant, of the Connecticut line, great-grandfather of the President who bore that name, were killed. The victims, dead and wounded alike, having been flung into Bloody Pond, it was thick and red for days, and tradition said that in after years it resumed its hue of crimson at sunset and held it until dawn. The captured, who were delivered to the Indians, had little to hope, for their white allies could not stay their savagery. Blind Rock was so called because the Indians brought a white man there, and tearing his eyes out, flung them into embers at the foot of the stone. Captives were habitually tortured, blazing splinters of pine being thrust into their flesh, their nails torn out, and their bodies slashed with knives before they went to the stake. An English prisoner was allowed to run the gauntlet here. They had already begun to strike at him as he sped between the lines, when he seized a pappoose, flung it on a fire, and, in the instant of confusion that followed, snatched an axe, cut the bonds of a comrade who had been doomed to die, and both escaped.

But the best-known history of this region is that of Rogers's Rock, or Rogers's Slide, a lofty precipice at the lower end of Lake George. Major Rogers did not toboggan down this rock in leather trousers, but his escape was no less remarkable than if he had. On March 13, 1758, while reconnoitring near Ticonderoga with two hundred rangers, he was surprised by a force of French and Indians. But seventeen of his men escaped death or capture, and he was pursued nearly to the brink of this cliff. During a brief delay among the red men, arising from the loss of his trail, he had time to throw his pack down the slide, reverse his snow-shoes, and go back over his own track to the head of a ravine before they emerged from the woods, and, seeing that his shoe-marks led to the rock, while none pointed back, they concluded that he had flung himself off and committed suicide to avoid capture. Great was their disappointment when they saw the major on the frozen surface of the lake beneath going at a lively rate toward Fort William Henry. He had gained the ice by way of the cleft in the rocks, but the savages, believing that he had leaped over the precipice, attributed his preservation to the Great Spirit and forbore to fire on him. Unconsciously, he had chosen the best possible place to disappear from, for the Indians held it in superstitious regard, believing that spirits haunted the wood and hurled bad souls down the cliff, drowning them in the lake, instead of allowing them to go to the happy hunting grounds. The major reached his quarters in safety, and lived to take up arms against the land of his birth when the colonies revolted, seventeen years later.

The Hudson and its Hills

THE FALLS AT COHOES

WHEN Occuna, a young Seneca, fell in love
with a girl whose cabin was near the present town of Cohoes, he behaved very much as Americans of a later date have done. He picked wild
flowers for her; he played on the bone pipe and
sang sentimental songs in the twilight; he roamed
the hills with her, gathering the loose quartz crystals that the Indians believed to be the tears of
stricken deer, save on Diamond Rock, in Lansing-
burgh, where they are the tears of Moneta, a bereaved mother and wife; and in fine weather they
went boating on the Mohawk above the rapids.
They liked to drift idly on the current, because it
gave them time to gaze into each other's eyes, and
to build air castles that they would live in in the
future. They were suddenly called to a realization
of danger one evening, for the stream had been
subtly drawing them on and on until it had them
in its power. The stroke of the paddle failed and
the air castles fell in dismal ruin. Sitting erect they
began their death-song in this wise:

Occuna: "Daughter of a mighty warrior, the
Manitou calls me hence. I hear the roaring of his
voice; I see the lightning of his glance along the
river; he walks in clouds and spray upon the
waters."

The Maiden: "Thou art thyself a warrior, O
Occuna. Hath not thine axe been often bathed in

93

blood? Hath the deer ever escaped thine arrow or the beaver avoided thy chase? Thou wilt not fear to go into the presence of Manitou."

Occuna: " Manitou, indeed, respects the strong. When I chose thee from the women of our tribe I promised that we should live and die together. The Thunderer calls us now. Welcome, O ghost of Oriska, chief of the invincible Senecas! A warrior and the daughter of a warrior come to join you in the feast of the blessed!"

The boat leaped over the falls, and Occuna, striking on the rocks below, was killed at once; but, as by a miracle, the girl fell clear of them and was whirled on the seething current to shoal water, where she made her escape. For his strength and his virtues the dead man was canonized. His tribe raised him above the regions of the moon, whence he looked down on the scenes of his youth with pleasure, and in times of war gave pleasant dreams and promises to his friends, while he confused the enemy with evil omens. Whenever his tribe passed the falls they halted and with brief ceremonials commemorated the death of Occuna.

FRANCIS WOOLCOTT'S NIGHT-RIDERS

IN Copake, New York, among the Berkshire Hills, less than a century ago, lived Francis Woolcott, a dark, tall man, with protruding teeth, whose sinister laugh used to give his neighbors a

The Hudson and its Hills

creep along their spines. He had no obvious trade or calling, but the farmers feared him so that he had no trouble in making levies : pork, flour, meal, cider, he could have what he chose for the asking, for had he not halted horses at the plow so that neither blows nor commands could move them for two hours? Had he not set farmer Raught's pigs to walking on their hind legs and trying to talk? When he shouted "Hup! hup! hup!" to farmer Williams's children, had they not leaped to the moulding of the parlor wainscot,—a yard above the floor and only an inch wide,—and walked around it, afterward skipping like birds from chair-back to chair-back, while the furniture stood as if nailed to the floor? And was he not the chief of thirteen night-riders, whose faces no man had seen, nor wanted to see, and whom he sent about the country on errands of mischief every night when the moon was growing old? As to moons, had he not found a mystic message from our satellite on Mount Riga, graven on a meteor?

Horses' tails were tied, hogs foamed at the mouth and walked like men, cows gave blood for milk. These night-riders met Woolcott in a grove of ash and chestnut trees, each furnished with a stolen bundle of oat straw, and these bundles Woolcott changed to black horses when the night had grown dark enough not to let the way of the change be seen. These horses could not cross streams of water, and on the stroke of midnight they fell to pieces and were oaten sheaves once more, but during their time of action they rushed through woods, bearing their riders safely, and tore like hurricanes across the fields, leaping bushes, fences, even trees, without effort. Never could traces be found of them the next day. At last the devil came to claim his own. Woolcott, who was ninety years old, lay sick and helpless in his cabin. Clergymen refused to see him, but two or three of his neighbors stifled their fears and went to the wizard's house to soothe his dying moments. With the night came storm, and with its outbreak the old man's face took on such a strange and horrible look that the watchers fell back in alarm. There was a burst of purple flame at the window, a frightful peal, a smell of sulphur, and Woolcott was dead. When the watchers went out the roads were dry, and none in the village had heard wind, rain, or thunder. It was the coming of the fiend.

POLLY'S LOVER

IN about the middle of this century a withered woman of ninety was buried from a now deserted house in White Plains, New York, Polly Carter the name of her, but " Crazy Polly " was what the neighbors called her, for she was eccentric and not fond of company. Among the belongings of her house was a tall clock, such as relic hunters prize, that ticked solemnly in a landing on the stairs.

The Hudson and its Hills

For a time, during the Revolution, the house stood within the British lines, and as her father was a colonel in Washington's army she was left almost alone in it. The British officers respected her sex, but they had an unpleasant way of running in unannounced and demanding entertainment, in the king's name, which she felt forced to grant. One rainy afternoon the door was flung open, then locked on the inside, and she found herself in the arms of a stalwart, handsome lieutenant, who wore the blue. It was her cousin and fiancé. Their glad talk had not been going long when there came a rousing summons at the door. Three English officers were awaiting admittance.

Perhaps they had seen Lawrence Carter go into the house, and if caught he would be killed as a spy. He must be hidden, but in some place where they would not think of looking. The clock! That was the place. With a laugh and a kiss the young man submitted to be shut in this narrow quarter, and throwing his coat and hat behind some furniture the girl admitted the officers, who were wet and surly and demanded dinner. They tramped about the best room in their muddy boots, talking loudly, and in order to break the effect of the chill weather they passed the brandy bottle freely. Polly served them with a dinner as quickly as possible, for she wanted to get them out of the house, but they were in no mood to go, and the bottle passed so often that before the dinner was over they were

7   97

noisy and tipsy and were using language that drove Polly from the room.

At last, to her relief, she heard them preparing to leave the house, but as they were about to go the senior officer, looking up at the landing, now dim in the paling light, said to one of the others, " See what time it is." The officer addressed, who happened to be the drunkest of the party, staggered up the stair and exclaimed, " The d——d thing's stopped." Then, as if he thought it a good joke, he added, " It'll never go again." Drawing his sabre he gave the clock a careless cut and ran the blade through the panel of the door; after this the three passed out. When their voices had died in distant brawling, Polly ran to release her lover. Something thick and dark was creeping from beneath the clock-case. With trembling fingers she pulled open the door, and Lawrence, her lover, fell heavily forward into her arms, dead. The officer was right: the clock never went again.

CROSBY, THE PATRIOT SPY

IT was at the Jay house, in Westchester, New York, that Enoch Crosby met Washington and offered his services to the patriot army. Crosby was a cobbler, and not a very thriving one, but after the outbreak of hostilities he took a peddler's outfit on his back and, as a non-combatant, of Tory sympathies, he obtained admission through the British

The Hudson and its Hills

lines. After his first visit to head-quarters it is
certain that he always carried Sir Henry Clinton's
passport in the middle of his pack, and so sure were
his neighbors that he was in the service of the
British that they captured him and took him to
General Washington, but while his case was up for
debate he managed to slip his handcuffs, which were
not secure, and made off. Clinton, on the other
hand, was puzzled by the unaccountable foresight
of the Americans, for every blow that he prepared
to strike was met, and he lost time and chance and
temper. As if the suspicion of both armies and
the hatred of his neighbors were not enough to
contend against, Crosby now became an object of
interest to the Skinners and Cowboys, who were
convinced that he was making money, somehow,
and resolved to have it.

The Skinners were camp-followers of the American troops and the Cowboys a band of Tories and
renegade British. Both factions were employed,
ostensibly, in foraging for their respective armies,
but, in reality, for themselves, and the farmers and
citizens occupying the neutral belt north of Manhattan Island had reason to curse them both impar-
tially. While these fellows were daring thieves,
they occasionally got the worst of it, even in the
encounters with the farmers, as on the Neperan,
near Tarrytown, where the Cowboys chased a
woman to death, but were afterward cut to pieces
by the enraged neighbors. Hers is but one of the

many ghosts that haunt the neutral ground, and the croaking of the birds of ill luck that nest at Raven rock is blended with the cries of her dim figure. Still, graceless as these fellows were, they affected a loyalty to their respective sides, and were usually willing to fight each other when they met, especially for the plunder that was to be got by fighting.

In October, 1780, Claudius Smith, " king of the Cowboys," and three scalawag sons came to the conclusion that it was time for Crosby's money to revert to the crown, and they set off toward his little house one evening, sure of finding him in, for his father was seriously ill. The Smiths arrived there to find that the Skinners had preceded them on the same errand, and they recognized through the windows, in the leader of the band, a noted brigand on whose head a price was laid. He was searching every crack and cranny of the room, while Crosby, stripped to shirt and trousers, stood before the empty fireplace and begged for that night to be left alone with his dying father.

" To hell with the old man !" roared the Skinner. " Give up your gold, or we'll put you to the torture," and he significantly whirled the end of a rope that he carried about his waist. At that moment the faint voice of the old man was heard calling from another room.

" Take all that I have and let me go !" cried Crosby, and turning up a brick in the fire-place he disclosed a handful of gold,—his life savings. The leader still tried to oppose his exit, but Crosby flung him to the floor and rushed away to his father, while the brigand, deeming it well to delay rising, dug his fingers into the hollow and began to extract the sovereigns. At that instant four muskets were discharged from without: there was a crash of glass, a yell of pain, and four of the Skinners rolled bleeding on the floor; two others ran into the darkness and escaped; their leader, trying to follow, was met at the threshold by the Smiths, who clutched the gold out of his hand and pinioned his elbows in a twinkling.

"I thought ye'd like to know who's got ye," said old Smith, peering into the face of the astonished and crestfallen robber, "for I've told ye many a time to keep out of my way, and now ye've got to swing for getting into it."

Within five minutes of the time that he had got his clutch on Crosby's money the bandit was choking to death at the end of his own rope, hung from the limb of an apple-tree, and, having secured the gold, the Cowboys went their way into the darkness. Crosby soon made his appearance in the ranks of the Continentals, and, though they looked askant at him for a time, they soon discovered the truth and hailed him as a hero, for the information he had carried to Washington from Clinton's camp had often saved them from disaster. He had survived attack in his own house through the falling out of rogues, and he survived the work and hazard of war through luck and a sturdy frame. Congress afterwards gave him a sum of money larger than had been taken from him, for his chief had commended him in these lines: "Circumstances of political importance, which involved the lives and fortunes of many, have hitherto kept secret what this paper now reveals. Enoch Crosby has for years been a faithful and unrequited servant of his country. Though man does not, God may reward him for his conduct.

"GEORGE WASHINGTON."

Associated with Crosby in his work of getting information from the enemy was a man named Gainos, who kept an inn on the neutral ground, that was often raided. Being assailed by Cowboys once, Gainos, with his tenant and stable-boys, fired at the bandits together, just as the latter had forced his front door, then stepping quickly forward he slashed off the head of the leader with a cutlass. The retreating crew dumped the body into a well on the premises, and there it sits on the crumbling curb o' nights looking disconsolately for its head.

It may also be mentioned that the Skinners had a chance to revenge themselves on the Cowboys for their defeat at the Crosby house. They fell upon the latter at the tent-shaped cave in Yonkers,—it is called Washington's Cave, because the general napped there on bivouac,—and not only routed them, but secured so much of their treasure that they were able to be honest for several years after.

The Hudson and its Hills

THE LOST GRAVE OF PAINE

FAILURE to mark the resting-places of great men and to indicate the scenes of their deeds has led to misunderstanding and confusion among those who discover a regard for history and tradition in this practical age. Robert Fulton, who made steam navigation possible, lies in an unmarked tomb in the yard of Trinity Church—the richest church in America. The stone erected to show where André was hanged was destroyed by a cheap patriot, who thought it represented a compliment to the spy. The spot where Alexander Hamilton was shot in the duel by Aaron Burr is known to few and will soon be forgotten. It was not until a century of obloquy had been heaped on the memory of Thomas Paine that his once enemies were brought to know him as a statesman of integrity, a philanthropist, and philosopher. His deistic religion, proclaimed in "The Age of Reason," is unfortunately no whit more independent than is preached in dozens of pulpits to-day. He died ripe in honors, despite his want of creed, and his mortal part was buried in New Rochelle, New York, under a large walnut-tree in a hay-field. Some years later his friends removed the body to a new grave in higher ground, and placed over it a monument that the opponents of his principles quickly hacked to pieces. Around the original grave there still remains a part of the old inclosure, and it was proposed to erect a suitable memorial on the spot, but the owner of the tract would neither give nor sell an inch of his land for the purpose of doing honor to the man. Some doubt has already been expressed as to whether the grave is beneath the monument or in the inclosure; and it is also asserted that Paine's ghost appears at intervals, hovering in the air between the two burial-places, or flitting back and forth from one to the other, lamenting the forgetfulness of men and wailing, " Where is my grave ? I have lost my grave !"

THE RISING OF GOUVERNEUR MORRIS

GOUVERNEUR MORRIS, American minister to the court of Louis XVI, was considerably enriched, at the close of the reign of terror, by plate, jewels, furniture, paintings, coaches, and so on, left in his charge by members of the French nobility, that they might not be confiscated in the sack of the city by the *sans culottes* ; for so many of the aristocracy were killed and so many went into exile or disguised their names, that it was impossible to find heirs or owners for these effects. Some of the people who found France a good country to be out of came to America, where adventurers had found prosperity and refugees found peace so many times before. Marshal Ney and Bernadotte are alleged to have served in the American army during the Revolution, and at Hogansburg, New York, the Reverend Eleazer Williams, an Episcopal missionary, who lies buried in the church-yard there, was declared to be the missing son of Louis XVI. The question, " Have we a Bourbon among us ?" was frequently canvassed ; but he avoided publicity and went quietly on with his pastoral work.

All property left in Mr. Morris's hands that had not been claimed was removed to his mansion at Port Morris, when he returned from his ministry, and he gained in the esteem and envy of his neighbors when the extent of these riches was seen. Once, at the wine, he touched glasses with his wife, and said that if she bore a male child that son should be heir to his wealth. Two relatives who sat at the table exchanged looks at this and cast a glance of no gentle regard on his lady. A year went by. The son was born, but Gouverneur Morris was dead.

It is the first night of the year 1817, the servants are asleep, and the widow sits late before the fire, her baby in her arms, listening betimes to the wind in the chimney, the beat of hail on the shutters, the brawling of the Bronx and the clash of moving ice upon it ; yet thinking of her husband and the sinister look his promise had brought to the faces of his cousins, when a tramp of horses is heard without, and anon a summons at the door. The panels are beaten by loaded riding-whips, and a man's voice cries, " Anne Morris, fetch us our cousin's will, or we'll break into the house and take it." The woman clutches the infant to her breast, but makes no answer. Again the clatter of the whips; but now a mist is gathering in the room, and a strange enchantment comes over her, for are not the lions breathing on the coat of arms above the door, and are not the portraits stirring in their frames?

They are, indeed. There is a rustle of robes and clink of steel and one old warrior leaps down, his armor sounding as he alights, and striking thrice his sword and shield together he calls on Gouverneur Morris to come forth. Somebody moves in the room where Morris died; there is a measured footfall in the corridor, with the clank of a scabbard keeping time; the door is opened, and on the blast that enters the widow hears a cry, then a double gallop, passing swiftly into distance. As she gazes, her husband appears, apparelled as in life, and with a smile he takes a candelabrum from the mantel and, beckoning her to follow, moves from room to room. Then, for the first time, the widow knows to what wealth her baby has been born, for the ghost discloses secret drawers in escritoires where money, title deeds, and gems are hidden, turns pictures and wainscots on unsuspected hinges, revealing shelves heaped with fabrics, plate, and lace; then, returning to the fireside, he stoops as if to kiss his wife and boy, but a bell strikes the first hour of morning and he vanishes into his portrait on the wall.

The Isle of Manhattoes and Nearby

The Isle of Manhattoes and Nearby

DOLPH HEYLIGER

NEW YORK was New Amsterdam when Dolph Heyliger got himself born there,—a graceless scamp, though a brave, good-natured one, and being left penniless on his father's death he was fain to take service with a doctor, while his mother kept a shop. This doctor had bought a farm on the island of Manhattoes—away out of town, where Twenty-third Street now runs, most likely—and, because of rumors that its tenants had noised about it, he seemed likely to enjoy the responsibilities of landholding and none of its profits. It suited Dolph's adventurous disposition that he should be deputed to investigate the reason for these rumors, and for three nights he kept his abode in the desolate old manor, emerging after daybreak in a lax and pallid condition, but keeping his own counsel, to the aggravation of the populace, whose ears were burning for his news.

Not until long after did he tell of the solemn tread that woke him in the small hours, of his door softly opening, though he had bolted and locked it, of a portly Fleming, with curly gray hair, reservoir boots, slouched hat, trunk and doublet, who entered

and sat in the arm-chair, watching him until the
cock crew. Nor did he tell how on the third night
he summoned courage, hugging a Bible and a cate-
chism to his breast for confidence, to ask the meaning of the visit, and how the Fleming arose, and
drawing Dolph after him with his eyes, led him
downstairs, went through the front door without
unbolting it, leaving that task for the trembling yet
eager youth, and how, after he had proceeded to a
disused well at the bottom of the garden, he vanished
from sight.

Dolph brooded long upon these things and dreamed
of them in bed. He alleged that it was in obedience
to his dreams that he boarded a schooner bound up
the Hudson, without the formality of adieu to his
employer, and after being spilled ashore in a gale at
the foot of Storm King, he fell into the company of
Anthony Vander Heyden, a famous landholder and
hunter, who achieved a fancy for Dolph as a lad
who could shoot, fish, row, and swim, and took him
home with him to Albany. The Heer had com-
modious quarters, good liquor, and a pretty daughter, and Dolph felt himself in paradise until led to
the room he was to occupy, for one of the first
things that he set eyes on in that apartment was a
portrait of the very person who had kept him awake
for the worse part of three nights at the bowerie in
Manhattoes. He demanded to know whose picture
it was, and learned that it was that of Killian Vander Spiegel, burgomaster and curmudgeon, who

The Isle of Manhattoes and Nearby

buried his money when the English seized New Amsterdam and fretted himself to death lest it should be discovered. He remembered that his mother had spoken of this Spiegel and that her father was the miser's rightful heir, and it now appeared that he was one of Heyden's forbears too. In his dream that night the Fleming stepped out of the portrait, led him, as he had done before, to the well, where he smiled and vanished. Dolph reflected, next morning, that these things had been ordered to bring together the two branches of the family and disclose the whereabouts of the treasure that it should inherit. So full was he of this idea that he went back to New Amsterdam by the first schooner, to the surprise of the Heer and the regret of his daughter.

After the truant had been received with execrations by the doctor and with delight by his mother, who believed that spooks had run off with him, and with astonishment, as a hero of romance, by the public, he made for the haunted premises at the first opportunity and began to angle at the disused well. Presently he found his hook entangled in something at the bottom, and on lifting slowly he discovered that he had secured a fine silver porringer, with lid held down by twisted wire. It was the work of a moment to wrench off the lid, when he found the vessel to be filled with golden pieces. His fishing that day was attended with such luck as never fell to an angler before, for there were other pieces of plate down there, all engraved with the Spiegel arms and all containing treasure.

By encouraging the most dreadful stories about the spot, in order to keep the people wide away from it, he accomplished the removal of his prizes bit by bit from their place of concealment to his home. His unaccounted absence in Albany and his dealings with the dead had prepared his neighbors for any change in himself or his condition, and now that he always had a bottle of schnapps for the men and a pot of tea for the women, and was good to his mother, they said that they had always known that when he changed it would be for the better,—at which his old detractors lifted their eyebrows significantly—and when asked to dinner by him they always accepted.

Moreover, they made merry when the day came round for his wedding with the little maid of Albany. They likewise elected him a member of the corporation, to which he bequeathed some of the Spiegel plate and often helped the other city fathers to empty the big punch-bowl. Indeed, it was at one of these corporation feasts that he died of apoplexy. He was buried with honors in the yard of the Dutch church in Garden Street.

THE KNELL AT THE WEDDING

A YOUNG New Yorker had laid such siege to the heart of a certain belle—this was back in the Knickerbocker days when people married for love—that everybody said the banns were as good as published; but everybody did not know, for one fine morning my lady went to church with another gentleman—not her father, though old enough to be —and when the two came out they were man and wife. The elderly man was rich. After the first paroxysm of rage and disappointment had passed, the lover withdrew from the world and devoted himself to study; nor when he learned that she had become a widow, with comfortable belongings derived from the estate of the late lamented, did he renew acquaintance with her, and he smiled bitterly when he heard of her second marriage to a young adventurer who led her a wretched life, but atoned for his sins, in a measure, by dying soon enough afterward to leave a part of her fortune unspent.

In the lapse of time the doubly widowed returned to New York, where she met again the lover of her youth. Mr. Ellenwood had acquired the reserve of a scholar, and had often puzzled his friends with his eccentricities; but after a few meetings with the object of his young affection he came out of his glooms, and with respectful formality laid again at her feet the heart she had trampled on forty years before. Though both of them were well on in life, the news of their engagement made little of a sensation. The widow was still fair; the wooer was quiet, refined, and courtly, and the union of their fortunes would assure a competence for the years that might be left to them. The church of

Myths and Legends

St. Paul, on Broadway, was appointed for the wedding, and it was a whim of the groom that his bride should meet him there. At the appointed hour a company of the curious had assembled in the edifice; a rattle of wheels was heard, and a bevy of bridesmaids and friends in hoop, patch, velvet, silk, powder, swords, and buckles walked down the aisle; but just as the bride had come within the door, out of the sunlight that streamed so brilliantly on the mounded turf and tombstones in the churchyard, the bell in the steeple gave a single boom.

The bride walked to the altar, and as she took her place before it another clang resounded from the belfry. The bridegroom was not there. Again and again the brazen throat and iron tongue sent out a doleful knell, and faces grew pale and anxious, for the meaning of it could not be guessed. With eyes fixed on the marble tomb of her first husband, the woman tremblingly awaited the solution of the mystery, until the door was darkened by something that made her catch her breath—a funeral. The organ began a solemn dirge as a black-cloaked cortege came through the aisle, and it was with amazement that the bride discovered it to be formed of her oldest friends,—bent, withered; paired, man and woman, as in mockery—while behind, with white face, gleaming eyes, disordered hair, and halting step, came the bridegroom, in his shroud.

"Come," he said, "let us be married. The coffins are ready. Then, home to the tomb."

The Isle of Manhattoes and Nearby

"Cruel!" murmured the woman.

"Now, Heaven judge which of us has been cruel. Forty years ago you took away my faith, destroyed my hopes, and gave to others your youth and beauty. Our lives have nearly run their course, so I am come to wed you as with funeral rites." Then, in a softer manner, he took her hand, and said, "All is forgiven. If we cannot live together we will at least be wedded in death. Time is almost at its end. We will marry for eternity. Come." And tenderly embracing her, he led her forward. Hard as was the ordeal, confusing, frightening, humiliating, the bride came through it a better woman.

"It is true," she said, "I have been vain and worldly, but now, in my age, the truest love I ever knew has come back to me. It is a holy love. I will cherish it forever." Their eyes met, and they saw each other through tears. Solemnly the clergyman read the marriage service, and when it was concluded the low threnody that had come from the organ in key with the measured clang of the bell, merged into a nobler motive, until at last the funeral measures were lost in a burst of exultant harmony. Sobs of pent feeling and sighs of relief were heard as the bridal party moved away, and when the new-made wife and husband reached the portal the bell was silent and the sun was shining.

Myths and Legends

ROISTERING DIRCK VAN DARA

IN the days when most of New York stood below Grand Street, a roistering fellow used to make the rounds of the taverns nightly, accompanied by a friend named Rooney. This brave drinker was Dirck Van Dara, one of the last of those swag-bellied topers that made merry with such solemnity before the English seized their unoffending town. It chanced that Dirck and his chum were out later than usual one night, and by eleven o'clock, when all good people were abed, a drizzle set in that drove the watch to sleep in doorways and left Broadway tenantless. As the two choice spirits reeled out of a hostelry near Wall Street and saw the lights go out in the tap-room windows they started up town to their homes in Leonard Street, but hardly had they come abreast of old St. Paul's when a strange thing stayed them: crying was heard in the churchyard and a phosphorescent light shone among the tombs. Rooney was sober in a moment, but not so Dirck Van Dara, who shouted, "Here is sport, friend Rooney. Let's climb the wall. If the dead are for a dance, we will take partners and show them how pigeons' wings are cut nowadays."

"No," exclaimed the other; "those must perish who go among the dead when they come out of their graves. I've heard that if you get into their clutches, you must stay in purgatory for a hundred years, and no priest can pray you out."

The Isle of Manhattoes and Nearby

"Bah! old wives' tales! Come on!" And pulling his friend with him, they were over the fence. "Hello! what have we here?" As he spoke a haggard thing arose from behind a tombstone, a witch-like creature, with rags falling about her wasted form and hair that almost hid her face. The twain were set a-sneezing by the fumes of sulphur, and Rooney swore afterwards that there were little things at the end of the yard with grinning faces and lights on the ends of their tails. Old Hollands are heady. Dirck began to chaff the beldam on her dilapidation, but she stopped his talk by dipping something from a caldron behind her and flinging it over both of her visitors. Whatever it was, it burned outrageously, and with a yell of pain they leaped the wall more briskly than they had jumped it the other way, and were soon in full flight. They had not gone far when the clock struck twelve.

"Arrah! there's a crowd of them coming after," panted Rooney. "Ave Mary! I've heard that if you die with witch broth being thrown over you, you're done for in the next world, as well as this. Let us get to Father Donagan's. Wow!"

As he made this exclamation the fugitives found their way opposed by a woman, who looked at them with immodest eyes and said, "Dirck Van Dara, your sire, in wig and bob, turned us Cyprians out of New York, after ducking us in the Collect. But we forgive him, and to prove it we ask you to our festival."

At the stroke of midnight the street before the
church had swarmed with a motley throng, that now
came onward, waving torches that sparkled like
stars. They formed a ring about Dirck and began
to dance, and he, nothing loth, seized the nymph
who had addressed him and joined in the revel. Not
a soul was out or awake except themselves, and no
words were said as the dance went wilder to strains
of weird and unseen instruments. Now and then
one would apply a torch to the person of Dirck,
meanly assailing him in the rear, and the smart of
the burn made him feat it the livelier. At last they
turned toward the Battery as by common consent,
and went careering along the street in frolic fashion.
Rooney, whose senses had thus far been pent in a
stupor, fled with a yell of terror, and as he looked
back he saw the unholy troop disappearing in the
mist like a moving galaxy. Never from that night
was Dirck Van Dara seen or heard of more, and the
publicans felt that they had less reason for living.

THE PARTY FROM GIBBET ISLAND

ELLIS ISLAND, in New York harbor, once
bore the name of Gibbet Island, because
pirates and mutineers were hanged there in chains.
During the times when it was devoted to this fell
purpose there stood in Communipaw the Wild
Goose tavern, where Dutch burghers resorted, to
smoke, drink Hollands, and grow fat, wise, and

The Isle of Manhattoes and Nearby

sleepy in each others' compaay. The plague of this inn was Yan Yost Vanderscamp, a nephew of the landlord, who frequently alarmed the patrons of the house by putting powder into their pipes and attaching briers beneath their horses' tails, and who naturally turned pirate when he became older, taking with him to sea his boon companion, an ill-disposed, ill-favored blackamoor named Pluto, who had been employed about the tavern. When the landlord died, Vanderscamp possessed himself of this property, fitted it up with plunder, and at intervals he had his gang ashore,—such a crew of singing, swearing, drinking, gaming devils as Communipaw had never seen the like of; yet the residents could not summon activity enough to stop the goings-on that made the Wild Goose a disgrace to their village. The British authorities, however, caught three of the swashbucklers and strung them up on Gibbet Island, and things that went on badly in Communipaw after that went on with quiet and secrecy.

The pirate and his henchmen were returning to the tavern one night, after a visit to a rakish-looking vessel in the offing, when a squall broke in such force as to give their skiff a leeway to the place of executions. As they rounded that lonely reef a creaking noise overhead caused Vanderscamp to look up, and he could not repress a shudder as he saw the bodies of his three messmates, their rags fluttering and their chains grinding in the wind.

Myths and Legends

"Don't you want to see your friends?" sneered Pluto. "You, who are never afraid of living men, what do you fear from the dead?"

"Nothing," answered the pirate. Then, lugging forth his bottle, he took a long pull at it, and holding it toward the dead felons, he shouted, "Here's fair weather to you, my lads in the wind, and if you should be walking the rounds to-night, come in to supper."

A clatter of bones and a creak of chains sounded like a laugh. It was midnight when the boat pulled in at Communipaw, and as the storm continued Vanderscamp, drenched to the skin, made quick time to the Wild Goose. As he entered, a sound of revelry overhead smote his ear, and, being no less astonished than in need of cordials, he hastened up-stairs and flung open the door. A table stood there, furnished with jugs and pipes and cans, and by light of candles that burned as blue as brimstone could be seen the three gallows-birds from Gibbet Island, with halters on their necks, clinking their tankards together and trolling forth a drinking-song.

Starting back with affright as the corpses hailed him with lifted arms and turned their fishy eyes on him, Vanderscamp slipped at the door and fell headlong to the bottom of the stairs. Next morning he was found there by the neighbors, dead to a certainty, and was put away in the Dutch churchyard at Bergen on the Sunday following. As the house was rifled and deserted by its occupants, it was hinted that the negro had betrayed his master to his fellow-buccaneers, and that he, Pluto, was no other than the devil in disguise. But he was not, for his skiff was seen floating bottom up in the bay soon after, and his drowned body lodged among the rocks at the foot of the pirates' gallows.

For a long time afterwards the island was regarded as a place that required purging with bell, book, and candle, for shadows were reported there and faint lights that shot into the air, and to this day, with the great immigrant station on it and crowds going and coming all the time, the Battery boatmen prefer not to row around it at night, for they are likely to see the shades of the soldier and his mistress who were drowned off the place one windy night, when the girl was aiding the fellow to escape confinement in the guard-house, to say nothing of Vanderscamp and his felons.

MISS BRITTON'S POKER

THE maids of Staten Island wrought havoc among the royal troops who were quartered among them during the Revolution. Near quarantine, in an old house,—the Austen mansion,—a soldier of King George hanged himself because a Yankee maid who lived there would not have him for a husband, nor any gentleman whose coat was of his color; and, until ghosts went out of fashion, his spirit, in somewhat heavy boots, with jingling spurs, often disturbed the nightly quiet of the place.

The conduct of a damsel in the old town of Richmond was even more stern. She was the granddaughter, and a pretty one, of a farmer named Britton; but though Britton by descent and name, she was no friend of Britons, albeit she might have had half the officers in the neighboring camp at her feet, if she had wished them there. Once, while mulling a cup of cider for her grandfather, she was interrupted by a self-invited myrmidon, who undertook, in a fashion rude and unexpected, to show the love in which he held her. Before he could kiss her, the girl drew the hot poker from the mug of drink and jabbed at the vitals of her amorous foe, burning a hole through his scarlet uniform and printing on his burly person a lasting memento of the adventure. With a howl of pain the fellow rushed away, and the privacy of the Britton family was never again invaded, at least whilst cider was being mulled.

THE DEVIL'S STEPPING-STONES

WHEN the devil set a claim to the fair lands at the north of Long Island Sound, his claim was disputed by the Indians, who prepared to fight for their homes should he attempt to serve his writ of ejectment. Parley resulted in nothing, so the bad one tried force, but he was routed in

The Isle of Manhattoes and Nearby

open fight and found it desirable to get away from the scene of action as soon as possible. He retreated across the Sound near the head of East River. The tide was out, so he stepped from island to island, without trouble, and those reefs and islands are to this day the Devil's Stepping-Stones. On reaching Throgg's Neck he sat down in a despairing attitude and brooded on his defeat, until, roused to a frenzy at the thought of it, he resolved to renew the war on terms advantageous entirely to himself. In that day Connecticut was free from rocks, but Long Island was covered with them; so he gathered all he could lay his hands on and tossed them at the Indians that he could see across the Sound near Cold Spring until the supply had given out. The red men who last inhabited Connecticut used to show white men where the missiles landed and where the devil struck his heel into the ground as he sprang from the shore in his haste to reach Long Island. At Cold Spring other footprints and one of his toes are shown. Establishing himself at Coram, he troubled the people of the country for many years, so that between the devil on the west and the Montauks on the east they were plagued indeed; for though their guard at Watch Hill, Rhode Island, and other places often apprised them of the coming of the Montauks, they never knew which way to look for the devil.

Myths and Legends

THE SPRINGS OF BLOOD AND WATER

A GREAT drought had fallen on Long Island, and the red men prayed for water. It is true that they could get it at Lake Ronkonkoma, but some of them were many miles from there, and, beside, they feared the spirits at that place: the girl who plied its waters in a phosphor-shining birch, seeking her recreant lover; and the powerful guardians that the Great Spirit had put in charge to keep the fish from being caught, for these fish were the souls of men, awaiting deliverance into another form. The people gathered about their villages in bands and besought the Great Spirit to give them drink. His voice was heard at last, bidding their chief to shoot an arrow into the air and to watch where it fell, for there would water gush out. The chief obeyed the deity, and as the arrow touched the earth a spring of sweet water spouted into the air. Running forward with glad cries the red men drank eagerly of the liquor, laved their faces in it, and were made strong again; and in memory of that event they called the place the Hill of God, or Manitou Hill, and Manet or Manetta Hill it is to this day. Hereabouts the Indians settled and lived in peace, thriving under the smile of their deity, making wampum for the inland tribes and waxing rich with gains from it. They made the canal from bay to sea at Canoe Place, that they might reach open water without dragging their boats across the sand-bars, and in other ways they proved themselves ingenious and strong.

When the English landed on the island they saw that the Indians were not a people to be trifled with, and in order to properly impress them with their superiority, they told them that John Bull desired a treaty with them. The officers got them to sit in line in front of a cannon, the nature of which instrument was unknown to them, and during the talk the gun was fired, mowing down so many of the red people that the survivors took to flight, leaving the English masters at the north shore, for this heartless and needless massacre took place at Whale's Neck. So angry was the Great Spirit at this act of cruelty and treachery that he caused blood to ooze from the soil, as he had made water leap for his thirsting children, and never again would grass grow on the spot where the murder had been done.

THE CRUMBLING SILVER

THERE is a clay bank on Little Neck, Long Island, where metallic nodules are now and then exposed by rain. Rustics declare them to be silver, and account for their crumbling on the theory that the metal is under a curse. A century ago the Montauks mined it, digging over enough soil to unearth these pellets now and again, and exchanging them at the nearest settlements for tobacco and rum. The seeming abundance of these lumps

of silver aroused the cupidity of one Gardiner, a
dweller in the central wilderness of the island, but
none of the Indians would reveal the source of their
treasure.   One day Gardiner succeeded in getting
an old chief so tipsy that, without realizing what he
was doing, he led the white man to the clay bed
and showed him the metallic spots glittering in the
sun.   With a cry of delight Gardiner sprang forward and tore at the earth with his fingers, while the
Indian stood by laughing at his eagerness.

Presently a shade crosssed the white man's face,
for he thought that this vast treasure would have to
be shared by others.   It was too much to endure.
He wanted all.   He would be the richest man on
earth.   Stealing behind the Indian as he stood sway-
ing and chuckling, he wrenched the hatchet from
his belt and clove his skull at a blow.   Then,
dragging the body to a thicket and hiding it under
stones and leaves, he hurried to his house for cart
and pick and shovel, and returning with speed he dug
out a half ton of the silver before sunset.   The cart
was loaded, and he set homeward, trembling with
excitement and conjuring bright visions for his future,
when a wailing sound from a thicket made him halt
and turn pale.   Noiselessly a figure glided from the
bush.   It was the Indian he had killed.   The form
approached the treasure, flung up its arm, uttered
a few guttural words ; then a rising wind seemed to
lift it from the ground and it drifted toward the
Sound, fading like a cloud as it receded.

The Isle of Manhattoes and Nearby

Full of misgiving, Gardiner drove to his home, and, by light of a lantern, transferred his treasure to his cellar. Was it the dulness of the candle that made the metal look so black? After a night of feverish tossing on his bed he arose and went to the cellar to gloat upon his wealth. The light of dawn fell on a heap of gray dust, a few brassy looking particles showing here and there. The curse of the ghost had been of power and the silver was silver no more. Mineralogists say that the nodules are iron pyrites. Perhaps so; but old residents know that they used to be silver.

THE CORTELYOU ELOPEMENT

IN the Bath district of Brooklyn stands Cortelyou manor, built one hundred and fifty years ago, and a place of defence during the Revolution when the British made sallies from their camp in Flatbush and worried the neighborhood. It was in one of these forays on pigs and chickens that a gallant officer of red-coats met a pretty lass in the fields of Cortelyou. He stilled her alarm by aiding her to gather wild-flowers, and it came about that the girl often went into the fields and came back with prodigious bouquets of daisies. The elder Cortelyou had no inkling of this adventure until one of his sons saw her tryst with the red-coat at a distance. Be sure the whole family joined him in remonstrance. As the girl declared that she would not forego the meetings with her lover, the father swore that she should never leave his roof again, and he tried to be as good, or bad, as his word. The damsel took her imprisonment as any girl of spirit would, but was unable to effect her escape until one evening, as she sat at her window, watching the moon go down and paint the harbor with a path of light. A tap at the pane, as of a pebble thrown against it, roused her from her revery. It was her lover on the lawn.

At her eager signal he ran forward with a light ladder, planted it against the window-sill, and in less than a minute the twain were running toward the beach; but the creak of the ladder had been heard, and grasping their muskets two of the men hurried out. In the track of the moon the pursuers descried a moving form, and, without waiting to challenge, they levelled the guns and fired. A woman's cry followed the report; then a dip of oars was heard that fast grew fainter until it faded from hearing. On returning to the house they found the girl's room empty, and next morning her slipper was brought in from the mud at the landing. Nobody inside of the American lines ever learned what that shot had done, but if it failed to take a life it robbed Cortelyou of his mind. He spent the rest of his days in a single room, chained to a staple in the floor, tramping around and around, muttering and gesturing, and sometimes startling the passer-by as he showed his white face and ragged beard at the window.

The Isle of Manhattoes and Nearby

VAN WEMPEL'S GOOSE

ALLOW us to introduce Nicholas Van Wempel, of Flatbush: fat, phlegmatic, rich, and henpecked. He would like to be drunk because he is henpecked, but the wife holds the purse-strings and only doles out money to him when she wants groceries or he needs clothes. It was New Year's eve, the eve of 1739, when Vrouw Van Wempel gave to her lord ten English shillings and bade him hasten to Dr. Beck's for the fat goose that had been bespoken. "And mind you do not stop at the tavern," she screamed after him in her shrillest tone. But poor Nicholas! As he went waddling down the road, snapping through an ice-crust at every step, a roguish wind—or perhaps it was one of the bugaboos that were known to haunt the shores of Gravesend Bay—snatched off his hat and rolled it into the very doorway of the tavern that he had been warned, under terrible penalties, to avoid.

As he bent to pick it up the door fell ajar, and a pungency of schnapps and tobacco went into his nostrils. His resolution, if he had one, vanished. He ordered one glass of schnapps; friends came in and treated him to another; he was bound to do as much for them; shilling by shilling the goose money passed into the till of the landlord. Nicholas was heard to make a muttered assertion that it was his own money anyhow, and that while he lived he would be the head of his own house; then the mut-

terings grew faint and merged into snores. When
he awoke it was at the low sound of voices in the
next room, and drowsily turning his head he saw
there two strangers,—sailors, he thought, from their
leather jackets, black beards, and the rings in their
ears. What was that they said? Gold? On the
marshes? At the old Flatlands tide-mill? The
talkers had gone before his slow and foggy brain
could grasp it all, but when the idea had fairly eaten
its way into his intellect, he arose with the nearest
approach to alacrity that he had exhibited in years,
and left the place. He crunched back to his home,
and seeing nobody astir went softly into his shed,
where he secured a shovel and lantern, and thence
continued with all consistent speed to the tumble-
down tide-mill on the marsh,—a trying journey for
his fat legs on a sharp night, but hope and schnapps
impelled him.

He reached the mill, and, hastening to the cellar,
began to probe in the soft, unfrozen earth. Presently his spade struck something, and he dug and
dug until he had uncovered the top of a canvas bag,
—the sort that sailors call a " round stern-chest."
It took all his strength to lug it out, and as he did
so a seam burst, letting a shower of gold pieces over
the ground. He loosed the band of his breeches,
and was filling the legs thereof with coin, when a
tread of feet sounded overhead and four men came
down the stair. Two of them he recognized as the
fellows of the tavern. They saw the bag, the

lantern, then Nicholas. Laden though he was with gold until he could hardly budge, these pirates, for such they were, got him up-stairs, forced him to drink hot Hollands to the success of their flag, then shot him through the window into the creek. As he was about to make this unceremonious exit he clutched something to save himself, and it proved to be a plucked goose that the pirates had stolen from a neighboring farm and were going to sup on when they had scraped their gold together. He felt the water and mud close over him; he struggled desperately; he was conscious of breathing more freely and of staggering off at a vigorous gait; then the power of all the schnapps seemed to get into his head, and he remembered no more until he heard his wife shrilling in his ears, when he sat up and found himself in a snow-bank close to his house, with a featherless goose tight in his grasp.

Vrouw Van Wempel cared less about the state of her spouse when she saw that he had secured the bird, and whenever he told his tale of the pirates she turned a deaf ear to him, for if he had found the gold why did he not manage to bring home a few pieces of it? He, in answer, asked how, as he had none of his own money, she could have come by the goose? He often told his tale to sympathetic ears, and would point to the old mill to prove that it was true.

Myths and Legends

THE WEARY WATCHER

BEFORE the opening of the great bridge sent commerce rattling up Washington Street in Brooklyn that thoroughfare was a shaded and beautiful avenue, and among the houses that attested its respectability was one, between Tillary and Concord Streets, that was long declared to be haunted. A man and his wife dwelt there who seemed to be fondly attached to each other, and whose love should have been the stronger because of their three children none grew to years. A mutual sorrow is as close a tie as a common affection. One day, while on a visit to a friend, the wife saw her husband drive by in a carriage with a showy woman beside him. She went home at once, and when the supposed recreant returned she met him with bitter reproaches. He answered never a word, but took his hat and left the house, never to be seen again in the places that had known him.

The wife watched and waited, daily looking for his return, but days lengthened into weeks, months, years, and still he came not. Sometimes she lamented that she had spoken hastily and harshly, thinking that, had she known all, she might have found him blameless. There was no family to look after, no wholesome occupation that she sought, so the days went by in listening and watching, until, at last, her body and mind gave way, and the familiar sight of her face, watching from a second floor win-

132

dow, was seen no longer. Her last day came. She had risen from her bed; life and mind seemed for a moment to be restored to her; and standing where she had stood so often, her form supported by a half-closed shutter and a grasp on the sash, she looked into the street once more, sighed hopelessly, and so died. It was her shade that long watched at the windows; it was her waxen face, heavy with fatigue and pain, that was dimly seen looking over the balusters in the evening.

THE RIVAL FIDDLERS

BEFORE Brooklyn had spread itself beyond Greenwood Cemetery a stone could be seen in Martense's Lane, south of that burial-ground, that bore a hoof mark. A negro named Joost, in the service of the Van Der Something-or-others, was plodding home on Saturday night, his fiddle under his arm. He had been playing for a wedding in Flatbush and had been drinking schnapps until he saw stars on the ground and fences in the sky; in fact, the universe seemed so out of order that he seated himself rather heavily on this rock to think about it. The behavior of the stars in swimming and rolling struck him as especially curious, and he conceived the notion that they wanted to dance. Putting his fiddle to his chin, he began a wild jig, and though he made it up as he went along, he was conscious of doing finely, when the boom of a bell sent a shiver down his spine. It was twelve o'clock, and here he was playing a dance tune on Sunday. However, the sin of playing for one second on the Sabbath was as great as that of playing all day; so, as long as he was in for it, he resolved to carry the tune to the end, and he fiddled away with a reckless vehemence. Presently he became aware that the music was both wilder and sweeter than before, and that there was more of it. Not until then did he observe that a tall, thin stranger stood beside him, and that he was fiddling too,—composing a second to Joost's air, as if he could read his thought before he put it into execution on the strings. Joost paused, and the stranger did likewise.

"Where de debble did you come frum?" asked the first. The other smiled.

"And how did you come to know dat music?" Joost pursued.

"Oh, I've known that tune for years," was the reply. "It's called 'The Devil's Joy at Sabbath Breaking.'"

"You're a liar!" cried the negro. The stranger bowed and burst into a roar of laughter. "A liar!" repeated Joost, "for I made up dat music dis very minute."

"Yet you notice that I could follow when you played."

"Humph! Yes, you can follow."

"And I can lead, too. Do you know the tune 'Go to the Devil and Shake Yourself?'"

"Yes; but I play second to nobody."

The Isle of Manhattoes and Nearby

" Very well, I'll beat you at any air you try."

" Done !" said Joost. And then began a contest that lasted until daybreak. The stranger was an expert, but Joost seemed to be inspired, and just as the sun appeared he sounded, in broad and solemn harmonies, the hymn of Von Catts:

> " Now behold, at dawn of day,
> Pious Dutchmen sing and pray."

At that the stranger exclaimed, " Well, that beats the devil !" and striking his foot angrily on the rock, disappeared in a flash of fire like a burst bomb. Joost was hurled twenty feet by the explosion, and lay on the ground insensible until a herdsman found him some hours later. As he suffered no harm from the contest and became a better fiddler than ever, it is supposed that the recording angel did not inscribe his feat of Sabbath breaking against him in large letters. There were a few who doubted his story, but they had nothing more to say when he showed them the hoof-mark on the rock. Moreover, there are fewer fiddlers among the negroes than there used to be, because they say that the violin is the devil's instrument.

WYANDANK

FROM Brooklyn Heights, or Ihpetonga, " high place of trees," where the Canarsie Indians made wampum or sewant, and where they contemplated the Great Spirit in the setting of the sun across the meeting waters, to Montauk Point, Long

Myths and Legends

Island has been swept by the wars of red men, and many are the tokens of their occupancy. A number of their graves were to be seen until within fifty years, as clearly marked as when the warriors were laid there in the hope of resurrection among the happy hunting grounds that lay to the west and south. The casting of stones on the death-spots or graves of some revered or beloved Indians was long continued, and was undoubtedly for the purpose of raising monuments to them, though at Monument Mountain, Massachusetts, Sacrifice Rock, between Plymouth and Sandwich, Massachusetts, and some other places the cairns merely mark a trail. Even the temporary resting-place of Sachem Poggatacut, near Sag Harbor, was kept clear of weeds and leaves by Indians who passed it in the two centuries that lapsed between the death of the chief and the laying of the road across it in 1846. This spot is not far from Whooping Boy's Hollow, so named because of a boy who was killed by Indians, and because the rubbing of two trees there in a storm gave forth a noise like crying. An older legend has it that this noise is the angry voice of the magician who tried to slay Wyandank, the "Washington of the Montauks," who is buried on the east end of the island. Often he led his men into battle, sounding the warwhoop, copied from the scream of the eagle, so loudly that those who heard it said that the Montauks were crying for prey.

It was while killing an eagle on Block Island, that

he might use the plumes for his hair, that this chief disclosed himself to the hostiles and brought on a fight in which every participant except himself was slain. He was secretly followed back to Long Island by a magician who had hopes of enlisting the evil ones of that region against him,—the giants that left their tracks in "Blood-stone Rock" and "Printed Rock," near Napeague, and such renegades as he who, having betrayed his people, was swallowed by the earth, his last agony being marked by a stamp of the foot that left its print on a slab near the Indian burial-ground at Kongonok. Failing in these alliances the wizard hid among the hollows of the moors, and there worked spells of such malice that the chief's hand lost steadiness in the hunt and his voice was seldom heard in council. When the haunt of this evil one was made known, a number of young men undertook to trap him. They went to the hills by night, and moved stealthily through the shrubbery until they were almost upon him; but his familiars had warned him of their approach, though they had wakened him only to betray him: for a cloud swept in from the sea, fell about the wretch, burst into flame, and rolled back toward the ocean, bearing him in the centre of its burning folds. Because of the cry he uttered the place long bore the name of Whooping Hollow, and it used to be said that the magician visited the scene of his ill-doing every winter, when his shrieks could be heard ringing over the hills.

Myths and Legends

MARK OF THE SPIRIT HAND

ANDOVER, New Jersey, was quaint and quiet in the days before the Revolution—it is not a roaring metropolis, even yet—and as it offered few social advantages there was more gathering in tap-rooms and more drinking of flip than there should have been. Among those who were not averse to a cheering cup were three boon companions, Bailey, Hill, and Evans, farmers of the neighborhood. They loved the tavern better than the church, and in truth the church folk did not love them well, for they were suspected of entertaining heresies of the most forbidden character. It was while they were discussing matters of belief over their glasses that one of them proposed, in a spirit of bravado, that whichever of the trio might be first to die should come back from the grave and reveal himself to the others —if he could—thus settling the question as to whether there was a future.

Not long after this agreement—for consent was unanimous—Hill departed this life. His friends lamented his absence, especially at the tavern, but they anticipated no attempt on his part to express the distinguished consideration that he had felt for his old chums. Some weeks passed, yet there was no sign, and the two survivors of the party, as they jogged homeward to the house where both lived, had begun to think and speak less frequently of the absent one. But one night the household was alarmed by a terrible cry. Bailey got a light and hurried to the bedside of his friend, whom he found deathly white and holding his chest as if in pain. "He has been here!" gasped Evans. "He stood here just now."

"Who?" asked Bailey, a creep passing down his spine.

"Hill! He stood there, where you are now, and touched me with a hand that was so cold—cold——" and Evans shivered violently. On turning back the collar of his shirt the impression of a hand appeared on the flesh near the shoulder: a hand in white, with one finger missing. Hill had lost a finger. There was less of taverns after that night, for Evans carried the token of that ghostly visit on his person until he, too, had gone to solve the great secret.

THE FIRST LIBERAL CHURCH

IN 1770 the brig Hand-in-Hand went ashore at Good Luck, New Jersey. Among the passengers on board the vessel, that it would perhaps be wrong to call ill fated, was John Murray, founder of Universalism in America. He had left England in despair, for his wife and children were dead, and so broken was he in his power of thought and purpose that he felt as if he should never preach again.

In fact, his rescue from the wreck was passive, on his part, and he suffered himself to be carried ashore, recking little whether he reached it or no. After

he had been for half an hour or so on the soil of
the new country, to which he had made his entrance
in so unexpected a manner, he began to feel hungry,
and set off afoot along the desolate beach. He came
to a cabin where an old man stood in a doorway
with a basket of fish beside him. "Will you sell
me a fish?" asked Murray.

"No. The fish is all yours. I expected you."

"You do not know me."

"You are the man who is to tell us of God."

"I will never preach of Him again."

"I built that log church yonder. Don't say that
you will not preach in it. Whenever a clergyman,
Presbyterian, Methody, or Baptist, came here, I
asked him to preach in my kitchen. I tried to get
him to stay; but no—he always had work elsewhere.
Last night I saw the brig driven on the bar, and a
voice said to me, 'In that ship is the man who will
teach of God. Not the old God of terrors, but
one of love and mercy. He has come through great
sorrow to do this work.' I have made ready for
you. Do not go away."

The minister felt a strange lifting in his heart.
He fell on his knees before the little house and
offered up a prayer. Long he staid in that place,
preaching gentle doctrines and ministering to the
men and women of that lonely village, and when
the fisherman apostle, Thomas Potter, died he left
the church to Murray, who, in turn, bequeathed it,
"free, for the use of all Christian people."

On and Near the Delaware

On and Near the Delaware

THE PHANTOM DRAGOON

THE height that rises a mile or so to the south of Newark, Delaware, is called Iron Hill, because it is rich in hematite ore, but about the time of General Howe's advance to the Brandywine it might well have won its name because of the panoply of war—the sullen guns, the flashing swords, and glistening bayonets—that appeared among the British tents pitched on it. After the red-coats had established camp here the American outposts were advanced and one of the pickets was stationed at Welsh Tract Church. On his first tour of duty the sentry was thrown into great alarm by the appearance of a figure robed from head to foot in white, that rode a horse at a charging gait within ten feet of his face. When guard was relieved the soldier begged that he might never be assigned to that post again. His nerves were strong in the presence of an enemy in the flesh—but an enemy out of the grave! Ugh! He would desert rather than encounter that shape again. His request was granted. The sentry who succeeded him was startled, in the small hours, by a rush of hoofs and the flash of a pallid form. He fired at it, and thought that he heard the sound of a mocking laugh come back.

Every night the phantom horseman made his rounds, and several times the sentinels shot at him without effect, the white horse and white rider showing no annoyance at these assaults. When it came the turn of a sceptical and unimaginative old corporal to take the night detail, he took the liberty of assuming the responsibilities of this post himself. He looked well to the priming of his musket, and at midnight withdrew out of the moonshine and waited, with his gun resting on a fence. It was not long before the beat of hoofs was heard approaching, and in spite of himself the corporal felt a thrill along his spine as a mounted figure that might have represented Death on the pale horse came into view; but he jammed his hat down, set his teeth, and sighted his flint-lock with deliberation. The rider was near, when bang went the corporal's musket, and a white form was lying in the road, a horse speeding into the distance. Scrambling over the fence, the corporal, reassured, ran to the form and turned it over: a British scout, quite dead. The daring fellow, relying on the superstitious fears of the rustics in his front, had made a nightly ride as a ghost, in order to keep the American outposts from advancing, and also to guess, from elevated points, at the strength and disposition of their troops. He wore a cuirass of steel, but that did not protect his brain from the corporal's bullet.

On and Near the Delaware

DELAWARE WATER GAP

THE Indian name of this beautiful region, Minisink, "the water is gone," agrees with the belief of geologists that a lake once existed behind the Blue Ridge, and that it burst its way through the hills at this point. Similar results were produced by a cataclysm on the Connecticut at Mount Holyoke, on the Lehigh at Mauch Chunk, and Runaway Pond, New Hampshire, got its name by a like performance. The aborigines, whatever may be said against them, enjoyed natural beauty, and their habitations were often made in this delightful region, their councils being attended by chief Tamanend, or Tammany, a Delaware, whose wisdom and virtues were such as to raise him to the place of patron saint of America. The notorious Tammany Society of New York is named for him. When this chief became old and feeble his tribe abandoned him in a hut at New Britain, Pennsylvania, and there he tried to kill himself by stabbing, but failing in that, he flung burning leaves over himself, and so perished. He was buried where he died. It was a princess of his tribe that gave the name of Lover's Leap to a cliff on Mount Tammany, by leaping from it to her death, because her love for a young European was not reciprocated.

There is a silver-mine somewhere on the opposite mountain of Minsi, the knowledge of its location having perished with the death of a recluse, who

coined the metal he took from it into valuable
though illegal dollars, going townward every winter
to squander his earnings. During the Revolution
"Oran the Hawk," a Tory and renegade, was
vexatious to the people of Delaware Valley, and a
detachment of colonial troops was sent in pursuit of
him. They overtook him at the Gap and chased
him up the slopes of Tammany, though he checked
their progress by rolling stones among them. One
rock struck a trooper, crushed him, and bore him
down to the base of a cliff, his blood smearing it in
his descent. But though he seemed to have eluded
his pursuers, Oran was shot in several places during
his flight, and when at last he cast himself into a
thicket, to rest and get breath, it was never to rise
again. His bones, cracked by bullets and gnawed
by beasts, were found there when the leaves fell.

THE PHANTOM DRUMMER

COLONEL HOWELL, of the king's troops,
was a gay fellow, framed to make women
false; but when he met the rosy, sweet-natured
daughter of farmer Jarrett, near Valley Forge, he
attempted no dalliance, for he fell too seriously in
love. He might not venture into the old man's
presence, for Jarrett had a son with Washington,
and he hated a red-coat as he did the devil; but the
young officer met the girl in secret, and they
plighted troth beneath the garden trees, hidden in

On and Near the Delaware

gray mist. As Howell bent to take his first kiss that night, a rising wind went past, bringing from afar the roll of a drum, and as they talked the drum kept drawing nearer, until it seemed at hand. The officer peered across the wall, then hurried to his mistress' side, as pale as death. The fields outside were empty of life.

Louder came the rattling drum; it seemed to enter the gate, pass but a yard away, go through the wall, and die in the distance. When it ceased, Howell started as if a spell had been lifted, laxed his grip on the maiden's hand, then drew her to his breast convulsively. Ruth's terror was more vague but no less genuine than his own, and some moments passed before she could summon voice to ask him what this visitation meant. He answered, "Something is about to change my fortunes for good or ill; probably for ill. Important events in my family for the past three generations have been heralded by that drum, and those events were disasters oftener than benefits." Few more words passed, and with another kiss the soldier scaled the wall and galloped away, the triple beat of his charger's hoofs sounding back into the maiden's ears like drum-taps. In a skirmish next day Colonel Howell was shot. He was carried to farmer Jarrett's house and left there, in spite of the old man's protest, for he was willing to give no shelter to his country's enemies. When Ruth saw her lover in this strait she was like to have fallen, but when she learned that it would take but a few days of quiet and care to restore him to health, she was ready to forgive her fellow-countrymen for inflicting an injury that might result in happiness for both of them.

It took a great deal of teasing to overcome the scruples of the farmer, but he gruffly consented to receive the young man until his hurt should heal. Ruth attended him faithfully, and the cheerful, manly nature of the officer so won the farmer's heart that he soon forgot the color of Howell's coat. Nor was he surprised when Howell told him that he loved his daughter and asked for her hand; indeed, it had been easy to guess their affection, and the old man declared that but for his allegiance to a tyrant he would gladly own him as a son-in-law. It was a long struggle between love and duty that ensued in Howell's breast, and love was victor. If he might marry Ruth he would leave the army. The old man gave prompt consent, and a secret marriage was arranged. Howell had been ordered to rejoin his regiment; he could not honorably resign on the eve of an impending battle, and, even had he done so, a long delay must have preceded his release. He would marry the girl, go to the country, live there quietly until the British evacuated Philadelphia, when he would return and cast his lot with the Jarrett household.

Howell donned citizen's dress, and the wedding took place in the spacious best room of the mansion, but as he slipped the ring on the finger of his bride the roll of a drum was heard advancing up the steps into the room, then on and away until all was still again. The young colonel was pale; Ruth clung to him in terror; clergymen and guests looked at each other in amazement. Now there were voices at the porch, the door was flung open, armed men entered, and the bridegroom was a prisoner. He was borne to his quarters, and afterward tried for desertion, for a servant in the Jarrett household, hating all English and wishing them to suffer, even at each other's hands, had betrayed the plan of his master's guest. The court-martial found him guilty and condemned him to be shot. When the execution took place, Ruth, praying and sobbing in her chamber, knew that her husband was no more. The distant sound of musketry reverberated like the roll of a drum.

THE MISSING SOLDIER OF VALLEY FORGE

DURING the dreadful winter of the American encampment at Valley Forge six or eight soldiers went out to forage for provisions. Knowing that little was to be hoped for near the camp of their starving comrades, they set off in the direction of French Creek. At this stream the party separated, and a little later two of the men were attacked by Tory farmers. Flying along the creek for some distance they came to a small cave in a bluff, and one of them, a young Southerner named Carrington, scrambled into it. His companion was not far behind, and was hurrying toward the cave, when he was arrested by a rumble and a crash : a block of granite, tons in weight, that had hung poised overhead, slid from its place and completely blocked the entrance. The stifled cry of despair from the living occupant of the tomb struck to his heart. He hid in a neighboring wood until the Tories had dispersed, then, returning to the cave, he strove with might and main to stir the boulder from its place, but without avail.

When he reached camp, as he did next day, he told of this disaster, but the time for rescue was believed to be past, or the work was thought to be too exhausting and dangerous for a body of men who had much ado to keep life in their own weak frames. It was a double tragedy, for the young man's sweetheart never recovered from the shock that the news occasioned, and on her tomb, near Richmond, Virginia, these words are chiselled : " Died, of a broken heart, on the 1st of March, 1780, Virginia Randolph, aged 21 years, 9 days. Faithful unto death." In the summer of 1889 some workmen, blasting rock near the falls on French Creek, uncovered the long-concealed cavern and found there a skeleton with a few rags of a Continental uniform. In a bottle beside it was an account, signed by Arthur L. Carrington, of the accident that had befallen him, and a letter declaring undying love for his sweetheart.

He had starved to death. The bones were neatly coffined, and were sent to Richmond to be buried beside those of the faithful Miss Randolph.

THE LAST SHOT AT GERMANTOWN

MANY are the tales of prophecy that have been preserved to us from war times. In the beginning of King Philip's war in Connecticut, in 1675, it was reported that the firing of the first gun was heard all over the State, while the drumbeats calling settlers to defence were audible eight miles away. Braddock's defeat and the salvation of Washington were foretold by a Miami chief at a council held in Fort Ponchartrain, on Detroit River, the ambush and the slaughter having been revealed to him in a dream. The victims of that battle, too, had been apprised, for one or two nights before the disaster a young lieutenant in Braddock's command saw his fellow-officers pass through his tent, bloody and torn, and when the first gun sounded he knew that it spoke the doom of nearly all his comrades. At Killingly, Connecticut, in the autumn before the outbreak of the Revolution, a distant roar of artillery was heard for a whole day and night in the direction of Boston, mingled with a rattle of musketry, and so strong was the belief that war had begun and the British were advancing, that the minute men mustered to await orders. It was afterward argued that these noises came from an explosion of meteors, a shower of these missiles being then in progress, invisible, of course, in the day-time. Just after the signing of the Declaration of Independence the royal arms on the spire of the Episcopal church at Hampton, Virginia, were struck off by lightning. Shortly before the surrender of Cornwallis a display of northern lights was seen in New England, the rays taking the form of cannon, facing southward. In Connecticut sixty-four of these guns were counted.

At the battle of Germantown the Americans were enraged by the killing of one of their men who had gone out with a flag of truce. He was shot from the windows of Judge Chew's house, which was crowded with British soldiers, and as he fell to the lawn, dyeing the peaceful emblem with his blood, at least one of the Continentals swore that his death should be well avenged. The British reinforcements, six-teen thousand strong, came hurrying through the street, their officers but half-dressed, so urgent had been the summons for their aid. Except for their steady tramp the place was silent; doors were locked and shutters bolted, and if people were within doors no sign of them was visible. General Agnew alone of all the troop seemed depressed and anxious. Turning to an aide as they passed the Mennonist graveyard, he said, "This field is the last I shall fight on."

An eerie face peered over the cemetery wall, a scarred, unshaven face framed in long hair and sur-

On and Near the Delaware

mounting a body clothed in skins, with the question, "Is that the brave General Gray who beat the rebels at Paoli?" One of the soldiers, with a careless toss of the hand, seemed to indicate General Agnew. A moment later there was a report, a puff of smoke from the cemetery wall, and a bullet whizzed by the head of the general, who smiled wanly, to encourage his men. Summary execution would have been done upon the stranger had not a body of American cavalry dashed against the red-coats at that moment, and a fierce contest was begun. When the day was over, General Agnew, who had been separated from his command in the confusion of battle, came past the graves again. Tired and depressed, he drew rein for a moment to breathe the sweet air, so lately fouled with dust and smoke, and to watch the gorgeous light of sunset. Again, like a malignant genius of the place, the savage-looking stranger arose from behind the wall. A sharp report broke the quiet of evening and awoke clattering echoes from the distant houses. A horse plunged and General Agnew rolled from his saddle, dead: the last victim in the strife at Germantown.

A BLOW IN THE DARK

THE Tory Manheim sits brooding in his farm-house near Valley Forge, and his daughter, with a hectic flush on her cheek, looks out into the twilight at the falling snow. She is worn and ill;

she has brought on a fever by exposure incurred that very day in a secret journey to the American camp, made to warn her lover of another attempt on the life of Washington, who must pass her father's house on his return from a distant settlement. The Tory knows nothing of this; but he starts whenever the men in the next room rattle the dice or break into a ribald song, and a frown of apprehension crosses his face as the foragers crunch by, half-bare-foot, through the snow. The hours go on, and the noise in the next room increases; but it hushes sud-denly when a knock at the door is heard. The Tory opens it, and trembles as a tall, grave man, with the figure of an athlete, steps into the fire-light and calmly removes his gloves. "I have been riding far," said he. "Can you give me some food and the chance to sleep for an hour, until the storm clears up?"

Manheim says that he can, and shuffling into the next room, he whispers, "Washington!" The girl is sent out to get refreshments. It is in vain that she seeks to sign or speak to the man who sits there so calmly before the fire, for her father is never out of sight or hearing. After Washington has finished his modest repast he asks to be left to himself for a while, but the girl is told to conduct him to the room on the left of the landing on the next floor.

Her father holds the candle at the foot of the stairs until he sees his guest enter; then he bids his

On and Near the Delaware

daughter go to her own bed, which is in the chamber on the right of the landing. There is busy whispering in the room below after that, and the dice box is shaken to see to whose lot it shall fall to steal up those stairs and stab Washington in his sleep. An hour passes and all in the house appear to be at rest, but the stairs creak slightly as Manheim creeps upon his prey. He blows his candle out and softly enters the chamber on the left. The men, who listen in the dark at the foot of the stair, hear a moan, and the Tory hurries back with a shout of gladness, for the rebel chief is no more and Howe's reward will enrich them for life.

Glasses are filled, and in the midst of the rejoicing a step is heard on the stair. Washington stands before them. In calm, deep tones he thanks the farmer for his shelter, and asks that his horse be brought to the door and his reckoning be made out. The Tory stares as one bereft. Then he rushes aloft, flings open the door of the room on the left, and gazes at the face that rests on the pillow,—a pillow that is dabbled with red. The face is that of his daughter. The name of father is one that he will never hear again in this world. The candle falls from his hand; he sinks to the floor; be his sin forgiven! Outside is heard the tramp of a horse. It is that of Washington, who rides away, ignorant of the peril he has passed and the sacrifice that averted it.

Myths and Legends

THE TORY'S CONVERSION

IN his firelit parlor, in his little house at Valley Forge, old Michael Kuch sits talking with his daughter. But though it is Christmas eve the talk has little cheer in it. The hours drag on until the clock strikes twelve, and the old man is about to offer his evening prayer for the safety of his son, who is one of Washington's troopers, when hurried steps are heard in the snow, there is a fumbling at the latch, then the door flies open and admits a haggard, panting man who hastily closes it again, falls into a seat, and shakes from head to foot. The girl goes to him. "John!" she says. But he only averts his face. "What is wrong with thee, John Blake?" asks the farmer. But he has to ask again and again ere he gets an answer. Then, in a broken voice, the trembling man confesses that he has tried to shoot Washington, but the bullet struck and killed his only attendant, a dragoon. He has come for shelter, for men are on his track already. "Thou know'st I am neutral in this war, John Blake," answered the farmer, "although I have a boy down yonder in the camp. It was a cowardly thing to do, and I hate you Tories that you do not fight like men; yet, since you ask me for a hiding-place, you shall have it, though, mind you, 'tis more on the girl's account than yours. The men are coming. Out—this way—to the spring-house. So!"

Before old Michael has time to return to his

On and Near the Delaware

chair the door is again thrust open, this time by
men in blue and buff. They demand the assassin,
whose footsteps they have tracked there through the
snow. Michael does not answer. They are about
to use violence when, through the open door, comes
Washington, who checks them with a word. The
general bears a drooping form with a blood splash on
its breast, and deposits it on the hearth as gently as
a mother puts a babe into its cradle. As the fire-
light falls on the still face the farmer's eyes grow
round and big; then he shrieks and drops upon his
knees, for it is his son who is lying there. Beside
him is a pistol; it was dropped by the Tory when
he entered. Grasping it eagerly the farmer leaps to
his feet. His years have fallen from him. With
a tiger-like bound he gains the door, rushes to the
spring-house where John Blake is crouching, his
eyes sunk and shining, gnawing his fingers in a craze
of dismay. But though hate is swift, love is swifter,
and the girl is there as soon as he. She strikes his
arm aside, and the bullet he has fired lodges in the
wood. He draws out his knife, and the murderer,
to whom has now come the calmness of despair,
kneels and offers his breast to the blade. Before
he can strike, the soldiers hasten up, and seizing
Blake, they drag him to the house—the little room
—where all had been so peaceful but a few minutes
before.

The culprit is brought face to face with Washington, who asks him what harm he has ever suffered

from his fellow countrymen that he should turn against them thus. Blake hangs his head and owns his willingness to die. His eyes rest on the form extended on the floor, and he shudders; but his features undergo an almost joyous change, for the figure lifts itself, and in a faint voice calls, " Father !" The young man lives. With a cry of delight both father and sister raise him in their arms. " You are not yet prepared to die," says Washington to the captive. " I will put you under guard until you are wanted. Take him into custody, my dear young lady, and try to make an American of him. See, it is one o'clock, and this is Christmas morning. May all be happy here. Come." And beckoning to his men he rides away, though Blake and his affianced would have gone on their knees before him. Revulsion of feeling, love, thankfulness and a latent patriotism wrought a quick change in Blake. When young Kuch recovered Blake joined his regiment, and no soldier served the flag more honorably.

LORD PERCY'S DREAM

LEAVING the dissipations of the English court, Lord Percy came to America to share the fortunes of his brethren in the contest then raging on our soil. His father had charged him with the delivery of a certain package to an Indian woman, should he meet her in his rambles through the western wilds, and, without inquiring into the nature of the gift or its occasion, he accepted the trust. At the battle of the Brandywine—strangely foretold by Quaker prophecy forty years before—he was detailed by Cornwallis to drive the colonial troops out of a graveyard where they had intrenched themselves, and though he set upon this errand with the enthusiasm of youth, his cheek paled as he drew near the spot where the enemy was waiting.

It was not that he had actual physical fear of the onset: he had dreamed a dream a few nights before, the purport of which he had hinted to his comrades, and as he rode into the clearing at the top of Osborn's Hill he drew rein and exclaimed, "My dream! Yonder is the graveyard. I am fated to die there." Giving a few of his effects to his brother officers, and charging one of them to take a message of love to his betrothed in England, he set his lips and rode forward.

His cavalry bound toward the scene of action and are within thirty paces of the cemetery wall, when from behind it rises a battalion of men in the green uniform of the Santee Rangers and pours a withering fire into the ranks. The shock is too great to withstand, and the red-coats stagger away with broken ranks, leaving many dead and wounded on the ground. Lord Percy is the coolest of all. He urges the broken columns forward, and almost alone holds the place until the infantry, a hundred yards behind, come up. Thereupon ensues one of those hand-to-hand encounters that are so rare in recent war, and that are the sorest test of valor and discipline. Now rides forward Captain Waldemar, chief of the rangers and a half-breed Indian, who, seeing Percy, recognizes him as an officer and engages him in combat. There is for a minute a clash of steel on steel; then the nobleman falls heavily to the earth—dead. His dream has come true. That night the captain Waldemar seeks out the body of this officer, attracted by something in the memory of his look, and from his bosom takes the packet that was committed to his care.

By lantern-light he reads, carelessly at first, then rapidly and eagerly, and at the close he looks long and earnestly at the dead man, and seems to brush away a tear. Strange thing to do over the body of an enemy! Why had fate decreed that they should be enemies? For Waldemar is the half-brother of Percy. His mother was the Indian girl that the earl, now passing his last days in England, had deceived with a pretended marriage, and the letters promise patronage to her son. The half-breed digs a grave that night with his own hands and lays the form of his brother in it.

SAVED BY THE BIBLE

IT was on the day after the battle of Germantown that Warner, who wore the blue, met his hated neighbor, the Tory Dabney, near that bloody field.

On and Near the Delaware

By a common impulse the men fell upon each other with their knives, and Warner soon had his enemy in a position to give him the death-stroke, but Dabney began to bellow for quarter. "My brother cried for quarter at Paoli," answered the other, "and you struck him to the heart."

"I have a wife and child. Spare me for their sakes."

"My brother had a wife and two children. Perhaps you would like to beg your life of them."

Though made in mockery, this proposition was caught at so earnestly that Warner at length consented to take his adversary, firmly bound, to the house where the bereaved family was living. The widow was reading the Bible to her children, but her grief was too fresh to gather comfort from it. When Dabney was flung into the room he grovelled at her feet and begged piteously for mercy. Her face did not soften, but there was a kind of contempt in the settled sadness of her tone as she said, "It shall be as God directs. I will close this Bible, open it at chance, and when this boy shall put his finger at random on a line, by that you must live or die."

The book was opened, and the child put his finger on a line: "That man shall die."

Warner drew his knife and motioned his prisoner to the door. He was going to lead him into the wood to offer him as a sacrifice to his brother's spirit.

"No, no!" shrieked the wretch. "Give me one more chance; one more! Let the girl open the book."

The woman coldly consents, and when the book is opened for the second time she reads, "Love your enemies." There are no other words. The knife is used, but it is to cut the prisoner's bonds, and he walks away with head hung down, never more to take arms against his countrymen. And glad are they all at this, when the husband is brought home—not dead, though left among the corpses at Paoli, but alive and certain of recovery, with such nursing as his wife will give him. After tears of joy have been shed she tells him the story of the Bible judgment, and all the members of the family fall on their knees in thanksgiving that the blood of Dabney is not upon their heads.

PARRICIDE OF THE WISSAHICKON

FARMER DERWENT and his four stout sons set off on an autumn night for the meeting of patriots at a house on the Wissahickon,—a meeting that bodes no good to the British encamped in Philadelphia, let the red-coats laugh as they will at the rag-tag and bob-tail that are joining the army of Mr. Washington in the wilds of the Skippack. The farmer sighs as he thinks that his younger son alone should be missing from the company, and wonders for the thousandth time what has become of the

On and Near the Delaware

boy. They sit by a rock that juts into the road to trim their lantern, and while they talk together they are startled by an exclamation. It is from Ellen, the adopted daughter of Derwent and the betrothed of his missing son. On the night that the boy stole away from his father's house he asked her to meet him in this place in a year's time, and the year is up to-night.

But it is not to meet him that she is hastening now: she has heard that the British have learned of the patriot gathering and will try to make prisoners of the company. Even as she tells of this there is a sound to the southward: the column is on the march. The farmer's eye blazes with rage and hate. "Boys," he says, "yonder come those who intend to kill us. Let them taste of their own warfare. Stand here in the shadow and fire as they pass this rock."

The troopers ride on, chuckling over their sure success, when there is a report of rifles and four of the red-coats are in the dust. The survivors, though taken by surprise, prove their courage by halting to answer the volley, and one of them springs from his saddle, seizes Derwent, and plunges a knife into his throat. The rebel falls. His blood pools around him. The British are successful, for two of the young men are bound and two of them have fallen, and there is a cheer of victory, but the trooper with the knife in his hand does not raise his voice. He bends above the farmer as still as one dead, until his captain claps him on the shoulder. As he rises, the prisoners start in wonder, for the face they see in the lantern-light is that of their brother, yet strange in its haggardness and its smear of blood on the cheek. The girl runs from her hiding-place with a cry, but stands in horror when her foot touches the gory pool in the road. The trooper opens his coat and offers her a locket. It contains her picture, and he has worn it above his heart for a year, but she lets it fall and sinks down, moaning. The soldier tears off his red coat, tramples it in the dust, then vaulting to his saddle he plunges into the river, fords it, and crashes through the underbrush on the other side. In a few minutes he has reached the summit of a rock that rises nearly a hundred feet above the stream. The horse halts at the edge, but on a fierce stab of the spur into his flank he takes the leap. With a despairing yell the traitor and parricide goes into eternity.

THE BLACKSMITH AT BRANDYWINE

TERRIBLE in the field at Brandywine was the figure of a man armed only with a hammer, who plunged into the ranks of the enemy, heedless of his own life, yet seeming to escape their shots and sabre cuts by magic, and with Thor strokes beat them to the earth. But yesterday war had been to him a distant rumor, a thing as far from his cottage at Dilworth as if it had been in Europe, but

On and Near the Delaware

he had revolted at a plot that he had overheard to capture Washington and had warned the general. In revenge the Tories had burned his cottage, and his wife and baby had perished in the flames. All day he had sat beside the smoking ruins, unable to weep, unable to think, unable almost to suffer, except dumbly, for as yet he could not understand it. But when the drums were heard they roused the tiger in him, and gaunt with sleeplessness and hunger he joined his countrymen and ranged like Ajax on the field. Every cry for quarter was in vain: to every such appeal he had but one reply,—his wife's name—Mary.

Near the end of the fight he lay beside the road, his leg broken, his flesh torn, his life ebbing from a dozen wounds. A wagoner, hasting to join the American retreat, paused to give him drink. "I've only five minutes more of life in me," said the smith. "Can you lift me into that tree and put a rifle in my hands?" The powerful teamster raised him to the crotch of an oak, and gave him the rifle and ammunition that a dying soldier had dropped there. A band of red-coats came running down the road, chasing some farmers. The blacksmith took careful aim; there was a report, and the leader of the band fell dead. A pause; again a report rang out, and a trooper sprawled upon the ground. The marksman had been seen, and a lieutenant was urging his men to hurry on and cut him down. There was a third report, and the lieutenant reeled forward into

the road, bleeding and cursing. " That's for Mary,"
gasped the blacksmith. The rifle dropped from his
hands, and he, too, sank lifeless against the boughs.

FATHER AND SON

IT was three soldiers, escaping from the rout of
Braddock's forces, who caught the alleged be-
trayer of their general and put him to the death.
They threw his purse of ill-gotten *louis d'or* into the
river, and sent him swinging from the edge of a
ravine, with a vine about his neck and a placard on
his breast. And so they left him.

Twenty years pass, and the war-fires burn more
fiercely in the vales of Pennsylvania, but, too old to
fight, the schoolmaster sits at his door near Chad's
Ford and smokes and broods upon the past. He
thinks of the time when he marched with Washington, when with two wounded comrades he returned
along the lonely trail; then comes the vision of a
blackening face, and he rises and wipes his brow.
" It was right," he mutters. " He sent a thousand
of his brothers to their deaths."

Gilbert Gates comes that evening to see the old
man's daughter: a smooth, polite young fellow, but
Mayland cannot like him, and after some short talk
he leaves him, pleading years and rheumatism, and
goes to bed. But not to sleep; for toward ten
o'clock his daughter goes to him and urges him to
fly, for men are gathering near the house—Tories,

she is sure,—and they mean no good. Laughing at her fears, but willing to relieve her anxiety, the old man slips into his clothes, goes into the cellar, and thence starts for the barn, while the girl remains for a few minutes to hide the silver.

He does not go far before Gates is at his elbow with the whispered words, "Into the stack—quick. They are after you." Mayland hesitates with distrust, but the appearance of men with torches leaves no time for talk. With Gilbert's help he crawls deep into the straw and is covered up. Presently a rough voice asks which way he has gone. Gilbert replies that he has gone to the wood, but there is no need for getting into a passion, and that on no account would it be advisable to fire the stack. "Won't we though?" cries one of the party. "We'll burn the rebel out of house and home," and thrusting his torch into the straw it is ablaze in an instant. The crowd hurries away toward the wood, and does not hear the stifled groan that comes out of the middle of the fire. Gates takes a paper from his pocket, and, after reading it for the last time, flings it upon the flame. It bears the inscription, "Isaac Gates, Traitor and Spy, hung by three soldiers of his majesty's army. Isaac Mayland."

From his moody contemplation he rouses with a start, for Mayland's daughter is there. Her eyes are bent on a distorted thing that lies among the embers, and in the dying light of the flames it seems to move. She studies it close, then with a cry of pain and terror she falls upon the hot earth, and her senses go out, not to be regained in woful years. With head low bowed, Gilbert Gates trudges away. In the fight at Brandywine next day, Black Samson, a giant negro, armed with a scythe, sweeps his way through the red ranks like a sable figure of Time. Mayland had taught him; his daughter had given him food. It is to avenge them that he is fighting. In the height of the conflict he enters the American ranks leading a prisoner—Gilbert Gates. The young man is pale, stern, and silent. His deed is known: he is a spy as well as a traitor, but he asks no mercy. It is rumored that next day he alone, of the prisoners, was led to a wood and lashed by arms and legs to a couple of hickory trees that had been bent by a prodigious effort and tied together by their tops. The lashing was cut by a rifle-ball, the trees regained their straight position with a snap like whips, and that was the way Gilbert Gates came to his end.

THE ENVY OF MANITOU

BEHIND the mountains that gloom about the romantic village of Mauch Chunk, Pennsylvania, was once a lake of clear, bright water, its winding loops and bays extending back for several miles. On one of its prettiest bits of shore stood a village of the Leni Lenape, and largest of its wigwams, most richly pictured without, most luxurious in its couching of furs within, was that of the young

On and Near the Delaware

chief, Onoko. This Indian was a man of great
size, strength, and daring. Single-handed he had
slain the bear on Mauch Chunk [Bear Mountain],
and it was no wonder that Wenonah, the fairest of
her tribe, was flattered when he sued for her hand,
and promptly consented to be his wife. It was
Onoko's fortune in war, the chase, and love that
roused the envy of Mitche Manitou.

One day, as the couple were floating in their
shallop of bark on the calm lake, idly enjoying the
sunshine and saying pretty things to each other, the
Manitou arose among the mountains. Terrible was
his aspect, for the scowl of hatred was on his face,
thunder crashed about his head, and fire snapped
from his eyes. Covering his right hand with his
invincible magic mitten, he dealt a blow on the hills
that made the earth shake, and rived them to a depth
of a thousand feet. Through the chasm thus created
the lake poured a foaming deluge, and borne with it
was the canoe of Onoko and Wenonah. One glance
at the wrathful face in the clouds above them and
they knew that escape was hopeless, so, clasping
each other in a close embrace, they were whirled
away to death. Manitou strode away moodily among
the hills, and ever since that time the Lehigh has
rolled through the chasm that he made. The memory
of Onoko is preserved in the name of a glen and
cascade a short distance above Mauch Chunk.

It is not well to be too happy in this world. It
rouses the envy of the gods.

THE LAST REVEL IN PRINTZ HALL

"YOUNG man, I'll give thee five dollars a week to be care-taker in Printz Hall," said Quaker Quidd to fiddler Matthews, on an autumn evening.

Young Matthews had just been taunting the old gentleman with being afraid to sleep on his own domain, and as the eyes of all the tavern loungers were on him he could hardly decline so flattering a proposition, so, after some hemming and hawing, he said he would take the Quaker at his word. He played but two or three more tunes that evening, did Peter Matthews, and played them rather sadly; then, as Quidd had finished his mulled cider and departed, he took his homeward way in thoughtful mood. Printz Hall stood in a lonely, weed-grown garden near Chester, Pennsylvania, and thither repaired Peter, as next day's twilight shut down, with a mattress, blanket, comestibles, his beloved fiddle, and a flask of whiskey. Ensconcing himself in the room that was least depressing in appearance he stuffed rags into the vacant panes, lighted a candle, started a blaze in the fireplace, and ate his supper.

"Not so bad a place, after all," mumbled Peter, as he warmed himself at the fire and the flask; then, taking out his violin, he began to play. The echo of his music emphasized the emptiness of the house, the damp got into the strings so that they sounded tubby, and there were unintentional quavers in the

On and Near the Delaware

melody whenever the trees swung against the windows and splashed them with rain, or when a distant
shutter fell a-creaking. Finally, he stirred the fire,
bolted the door, snuffed his candle, took a courageous
pull at the liquor, flung off his coat and shoes, rolled
his blanket around him, stretched himself on the
mattress, and fell asleep. He was awakened by—
well, he could not say what, exactly, only he became
suddenly as wide awake as ever he had been in his
life, and listened for some sound that he knew was
going to come out of the roar of the wind and the
slamming, grating, and whistling about the house.
Yes, there it was: a tread and a clank on the stair.
The door, so tightly bolted, flew open, and there
entered a dark figure with steeple-crowned hat, cloak,
jack-boots, sword, and corselet. The terrified fiddler
wanted to howl, but his voice was gone. "I am
Peter Printz, governor-general of his Swedish Majesty's American colonies, and builder of this house,"
said the figure. "'Tis the night of the autumnal
equinox, when my friends meet here for revel. Take
thy fiddle and come. Play, but speak not."

And whether he wished or no, Peter was drawn
to follow the figure, which he could make out by
the phosphor gleam of it. Down-stairs they went,
doors swinging open before them, and along cor-
ridors that clanged to the stroke of the spectre's
boot heels. Now they came to the ancient recep-
tion-room, and as they entered it Peter was dazzled.
The floor was smooth with wax, logs snapped in

the fireplace, though the flame was somewhat blue, the old hangings and portraits looked fresh, and in the light of wax candles a hundred people, in the brave array of old times, walked, courtesied, and seemed to laugh and talk together. As the fiddler appeared, every eye was turned on him in a disquieting way, and when he addressed himself to his bottle, from every throat came a hollow laugh. Finding his way to a chair he sank into it and put his instrument in position. At the first note the couples took hands, and as he struck into a jig they began to circle swiftly, leaping wondrous high.

Faster went the music, for the whiskey was at work in Peter's noddle, and wilder grew the dance. It was as if the storm had come in through the windows and was blowing these people hither and yon, around and around. The fiddler vaguely wondered at himself, for he had never played so well, though he had never heard the tune before. Now loomed Governor Printz in the middle of the room, and extending his hand he ordered the dance to cease. "Thou hast played well, fiddler," he said, "and shalt be paid." Then, at his signal, came two negro men tugging at a strong box that Printz unlocked. It was filled with gold pieces. "Hold thy fiddle bag," commanded the governor, and Peter did so, watching, open mouthed, the transfer of a double handful of treasure from box to sack. Another such handful followed, and another. At the fourth Peter could no longer contain himself. He

forgot the injunction not to speak, and shouted glee-
fully, "Lord Harry! Here's luck!"

There was a shriek of demon laughter, the scene
was lost in darkness, and Peter fell insensible. In
the morning a tavern-haunting friend, anxious to
know if Peter had met with any adventure, entered
the house and went cautiously from room to room,
calling on the watcher to show himself. There
was no response. At last he stumbled on the
whiskey bottle, empty, and knew that Peter must
be near. Sure enough, there he lay in the great
room, with dust and mould thick on everything, and
his fiddle smashed into a thousand pieces. Peter on
being awakened looked ruefully about him, then
sprang up and eagerly demanded his money. "What
money?" asked his friend. The fiddler clutched at
his green bag, opened it, shook it; there was nothing.
Nor was there any delay in Peter's exit from that
mansion, and when, twenty-four hours after, the
house went up in flames, he averred that the ghosts
had set it afire, and that he knew where they brought
their coals from.

THE TWO RINGS

GABRIELLE DE ST. PIERRE, daughter of
the commandant of Fort Le Bœuf, now
Waterford, Pennsylvania, that the French had set
up on the Ohio River, was Parisian by birth and
training, but American by choice, for she had en-

joyed on this lonesome frontier a freedom equal to that of the big-handed, red-faced half-breeds, and she was as wild as an Indian in her sports. Returning from a hunt, one day, she saw three men advancing along the trail, and, as it was easy to see that they were not Frenchmen, her guide slipped an arrow to the cord and discharged it; but Gabrielle was as quick as he, for she struck the missile as it was leaving the bow and it quivered harmlessly into a beech. The younger of the men who were advancing—he was Harry Fairfax, of Virginia—said to his chief, "Another escape for you, George. Heaven sent one of its angels to avert that stroke."

Washington, for it was he, answered lightly, and, as no other hostile demonstrations were made, the new-comers pressed on to the fort, where St. Pierre received them cordially, though he knew that their errand was to claim his land on behalf of the English and urge the French to retire to the southwest. The days that were spent in futile negotiation passed all too swiftly for Fairfax, for he had fallen in love with Gabrielle. She would not consent to a betrothal until time had tried his affection, but as a token of friendship she gave him a stone circlet of Indian manufacture, and received in exchange a ring that had been worn by the mother of Fairfax.

After the diplomats had returned the English resolved to enforce their demand with arms, and Fairfax was one of the first to be despatched to the front. Early in the campaign his company engaged the enemy near the Ohio River, and in the heat of battle he had time to note and wonder at the strange conduct of one of the French officers, a mere stripling, who seemed more concerned to check the fire of his men than to secure any advantage in the fight. Presently the French gave way, and with a cheer the English ran forward to claim the field, the ruder spirits among them at once beginning to plunder the wounded. A cry for quarter drew Fairfax with a bound to the place whence it came, and, dashing aside a pilfering soldier, he bent above a slight form that lay extended on the earth: the young officer whose strange conduct had so surprised him. In another moment he recognized his mother's ring on one of the slender hands. It was Gabrielle. Her father had perished in the fight, but she had saved her lover.

In due time she went with her affianced to his home in Williamsburg, Virginia, and became mistress of the Fairfax mansion. But she never liked the English, as a people, and when, in later years, two sturdy sons of hers asked leave to join the Continental army, she readily consented.

FLAME SCALPS OF THE CHARTIERS

BEFORE Pittsburg had become worthy to be called a settlement, a white man rowed his boat to the mouth of Chartiers creek, near that present city. He was seeking a place in which to make his home, and a little way up-stream, where were timber, water, and a southern slope, he marked a " tomahawk claim," and set about clearing the land. Next year his wife, two children, and his brother came to occupy the cabin he had built, and for a long time all went happily, but on returning from a long hunt the brothers found the little house in ashes and the charred remains of its occupants in the ruins. Though nearly crazed by this catastrophe they knew that their own lives were in hourly peril, and they wished to live until they could punish the savages for this crime. After burying the bodies, they started east across the hills, leaving a letter on birch bark in a cleft stick at the mouth of Chartiers creek, in which the tragedy was recounted.

This letter was afterward found by trappers. The men themselves were never heard from, and it is believed that they, too, fell at the hands of the Indians. Old settlers used to affirm that on summer nights the cries of the murdered innocents could be heard in the little valley where the cabin stood, and when storms were coming up these cries were often blended with the yells of savages. More impressive are the death lights—the will-o'-the-wisps—that wander over the scene of the tragedy, and up and down the neighboring slopes. These apparitions are said to be the spirits of husband and wife seeking each other, or going together in search of their children ; but some declare that in their upward streaming rays it can readily be seen that they are the scalps of the slain. Two of them have a golden hue, and these are the scalps of the children. From beneath them drops of red seem to distil on the grass and are found to have bedewed the flowers on the following morning.

THE CONSECRATION OF WASHINGTON

IN 1773 some of the Pietist monks were still living in their rude monastery whose ruins are visible on the banks of the Wissahickon. Chief among these mystics was an old man who might have enjoyed the wealth and distinction warranted by a title had he chosen to remain in Germany, but he had forsworn vanities, and had come to the new world to pray, to rear his children, and to live a simple life. Some said he was an alchemist, and many believed him to be a prophet. The infrequent wanderer beside the romantic river had seen lights burning in the window of his cell and had heard the solemn sound of song and prayer. On a winter night, when snow lay untrodden about the building and a sharp air stirred in the trees with a sound like harps, the old man sat in a large room of the place, with his son and daughter, waiting. For a prophecy had run that on that night, at the third hour of morning, the Deliverer would present himself. In a dream was heard a voice, saying, " I will send a deliverer to the new world who shall save my people from bondage, as my Son saved them from spiritual death." The night wore on in prayer and meditation, and the hours tolled heavily across the frozen wilderness, but, at the stroke of three, steps were heard in the snow and the door swung open. The man who entered was of great stature, with a calm, strong face, a powerful frame, and a manner of dignity and grace.

"Friends, I have lost my way," said he. "Can you direct me?"

The old man started up in a kind of rapture. "You have not lost your way," he cried, "but found it. You are called to a great mission. Kneel at this altar and receive it."

The stranger looked at the man in surprise and a doubt passed over his face. "Nay, I am not mad," urged the recluse, with a slight smile. "Listen: to-night, disturbed for the future of your country, and unable to sleep, you mounted horse and rode into the night air to think on the question that cannot be kept out of your mind, Is it lawful for the subject to draw sword against his king? The horse wandered, you knew and cared not whither, until he brought you here."

"How do you know this?" asked the stranger, in amazement.

"Be not surprised, but kneel while I anoint thee deliverer of this land."

Moved and impressed, the man bowed his knee before one of his fellows for the first time in his life. The monk touched his finger with oil, and laying it on the brow of the stranger said, "Do you promise, when the hour shall strike, to take the sword in defence of your country? Do you promise, when you shall see your soldiers suffer for bread and fire, and when the people you have led to victory shall bow before you, to remember that you are but the minister of God in the work of a nation's freedom?"

With a new light burning in his eyes, the stranger bent his head.

"Then, in His name, I consecrate thee deliverer of this oppressed people. When the time comes, go forth to victory, for, as you are faithful, be sure that God will grant it. Wear no crown, but the blessings and honor of a free people, save this." As he finished, his daughter, a girl of seventeen, came forward and put a wreath of laurel on the brow of the kneeling man. "Rise," continued the prophet, "and take my hand, which I have never before offered to any man, and accept my promise to be faithful to you and to this country, even if it cost my life."

As he arose, the son of the priest stepped to him and girt a sword upon his hip, and the old man held up his hands in solemn benediction. The stranger laid his hand on the book that stood open on the altar and kissed the hilt of his sword. "I will keep the faith," said he. At dawn he went his way again, and no one knew his name, but when the fires of battle lighted the western world America looked to him for its deliverance from tyranny. Years later it was this spot that he revisited, alone, to pray, and here Sir William Howe offered to him, in the name of his king, the title of regent of America. He took the parchment and ground it into a rag in the earth at his feet. For this was Washington.

MARION

BLOOMING and maidenly, though she dressed in leather and used a rifle like a man, was Marion, grand-daughter of old Abraham, who counted his years as ninety, and who for many of those years had lived with his books in the tidy cabin where the Youghiogheny and Monongahela come together. This place stood near the trail along which Braddock marched to his defeat, and it was one of the stragglers from this command, a bony half-breed with red hair, called Red Wolf, that knocked at the door and asked for water. Seeing no one but Marion he ventured in, and would have tried not only to make free with the contents of the little house but would have kissed the girl as well, only that she seized her rifle and held him at bay. Still, the fellow would have braved a shot, had not a young officer in a silver-laced uniform glanced through the open door in passing and discovered the situation. He doffed his chapeau to Marion, then said sternly to the rogue, "Retire. Your men are waiting for you." Red Wolf slunk away, and Washington, for it was he, begged that he might rest for a little time under the roof.

This request was gladly complied with, both by the girl and by her grandfather, who presently appeared, and the fever that threatened the young soldier was averted by a day of careful nursing. Marion's innate refinement, her gentleness, her vivacity, could not fail to interest Washington, and the vision of her face was with him for many a day. He promised to return, then he rode forward and caught up with the troops. He survived the battle in which seven hundred of his comrades were shot or tomahawked and scalped. One Indian fired at him eleven times, and five of the bullets scratched him; after that the savage forbore, believing that the officer was under Manitou's protection. When the retreating column approached the place where Marion lived he hastened on in advance to see her. The cabin was in ashes. He called, but there was no answer. When he turned away, with sad and thoughtful mien, a brown tress was wrapped around his finger, and in his cabinet he kept it until his death, folded in a paper marked " Marion, July 11, 1755."

Tales of Puritan Land

Tales of Puritan Land

EVANGELINE

THE seizure by England of the country that soon afterward was rechristened Nova Scotia was one of the saddest events in history. The land was occupied by a good and happy people who had much faith and few laws, plenty to eat and drink, no tax collectors nor magistrates,—in brief, a people who were entitled to call themselves Arcadians, rather than Acadians, for they made their land an Arcady. Upon them swooped the British ships, took them unarmed, crowded them aboard their transports, —often separating husband and wife, parents and children,—scattered them far and wide, beyond hope of return, and set up the cross of St. George on the ruins of prosperity and peace. On the shore of the Basin of Minas can still be traced the foundations of many homes that were perforce deserted at that time, and among them are the ruins of Grand Pré.

Here lived Evangeline Bellefontaine and Gabriel Lajeunesse, who were betrothed with the usual rejoicings just before the coming of the English. They had expected, when their people were arrested, to be sent away together; but most of the men were kept under guard, and Gabriel was at sea, bound neither he nor she knew whither, when Evangeline found herself in her father's house alone, for grief and excitement had been more than her aged parent could bear, and he was buried at the shore just before the women of the place were crowded on board of a transport. As the ship set off her sorrowing passengers looked behind them to see their homes going up in flame and smoke, and Acadia knew them no more. The English had planned well to keep these people from coming together for conspiracy or revenge: they scattered them over all America, from Newfoundland to the southern savannas.

Evangeline was not taken far away, only to New England; but without Gabriel all lands were drear, and she set off in the search for him, working here and there, sometimes looking timidly at the head-stones on new graves, then travelling on. Once she heard that he was a *coureur des bois* on the prairies, again that he was a *voyageur* in the Louisiana low-lands; but those of his people who kept near her inclined to jest at her faith and urged her to marry Leblanc, the notary's son, who truly loved her. To these she only replied, " I cannot."

Down the Ohio and Mississippi she went—on a raft—with a little band of those who were seeking the French settlements, where the language, religion, and simplicity of life recalled Acadia. They found it on the banks of the Teche, and they reached the house of the herdsman Gabriel on the day that he had departed for the north to seek Evangeline. She and the good priest who had been her stay in a year of sorrow turned back in pursuit, and for weary months, over prairie and through forest, skirting mountain and morass, going freely among savages, they followed vain clues, and at last arrived in Philadelphia. Broken in spirit then, but not less sweet of nature for the suffering that she had known, she who had been named for the angels became a minister of mercy, and in the black robe of a nun went about with comforts to the sick and poor. A pestilence was sweeping through the city, and those who had no friends nor attendants were taken to the almshouse, whither, as her way was, Evangeline went on a soft Sabbath morning to calm the fevered and brighten the hearts of the dying.

Some of the patients of the day before had gone and new were in their places. Suddenly she turned white and sank on her knees at a bedside, with a cry of " Gabriel, my beloved !" breathed into the ears of a prematurely aged man who lay gasping in death before her. He came out of his stupor, slowly, and tried to speak her name. She drew his head to her bosom, kissed him, and for one moment they were happy. Then the light went out of his eyes and the warmth from his heart. She pressed his eyelids down and bowed her head, for her way was plainer now, and she thanked God that it was so.

Myths and Legends

THE SNORING OF SWUNKSUS

THE original proprietor of Deer Isle, off the coast of Maine—at least, the one who was in possession one hundred and thirty years ago—had the liquid name of Swunksus. His name was not the only liquid thing in the neighborhood, however, for, wherever Swunksus was, fire-water was not far. Shortly before the Revolution a renegade from Boston, one Conary, moved up to the island and helped himself to as much of it as he chose, but the longer he lived there the more he wanted. Swunksus was willing enough to divide his domain with the white intruder, but Conary was not satisfied with half. He did not need it all; he just wanted it. Moreover, he grew quarrelsome and was continually nagging poor Swunksus, until at last he forced the Indian to accept a challenge, not to immediate combat, but to fight to the death should they meet thereafter.

The red man retired to his half of the island and hid among the bushes near his home to await the white man, but in this little fastness he discovered a jug of whiskey that either fate or Conary had placed there. Before an hour was over he was "as full and mellow as a harvest moon," and it was then that his enemy appeared. There was no trouble in finding Swunksus, for he was snoring like a fog horn, and walking boldly up to him, Conary blew his head off with a load of slugs. Then he

188

took possession of the place and lived happily ever after. Swunksus takes his deposition easily, for, although he has more than once paraded along the beaches, his ghost spends most of the time in slumber, and terrific snores have been heard proceeding from the woods in daylight.

THE LEWISTON HERMIT

ON an island above the falls of the Androscoggin, at Lewiston, Maine, lived a white recluse at the beginning of the eighteenth century. The natives, having had good reason to mistrust all palefaces, could think no good of the man who lived thus among but not with them. Often they gathered at the bank and looked across at his solitary candle twinkling among the leaves, and wondered what manner of evil he could be planning against them. Wherever there are many conspirators one will be a gabbler or a traitor; so, when the natives had resolved on his murder, he, somehow, learned of their intent and set himself to thwart it. So great was their fear of this lonely man, and of the malignant powers he might conjure to his aid, that nearly fifty Indians joined the expedition, to give each other courage.

Their plan was to go a little distance up the river and come down with the current, thus avoiding the dip of paddles that he might hear in a direct crossing. When it was quite dark they set off, and keeping headway on their canoes aimed them toward the light that glimmered above the water. But the cunning hermit had no fire in his cabin that night. It was burning on a point below his shelter, and from his hiding-place among the rocks he saw their fleet, as dim and silent as shadows, go by him on the way to the misguiding beacon.

Presently a cry arose. The savages had passed the point of safe sailing; their boats had become unmanageable. Forgetting their errand, their only hope now was to save themselves, but in vain they tried to reach the shore: the current was whirling them to their doom. Cries and death-songs mingled with the deepening roar of the waters, the light barks reached the cataract and leaped into the air. Then the night was still again, save for the booming of the flood. Not one of the Indians who had set out on this errand of death survived the hermit's stratagem.

THE DEAD SHIP OF HARPSWELL

AT times the fisher-folk of Maine are startled to see the form of a ship, with gaunt timbers showing through the planks, like lean limbs through rents in a pauper's garb, float shoreward in the sunset. She is a ship of ancient build, with tall masts and sails of majestic spread, all torn; but what is her name, her port, her flag, what harbor she is trying to make, no man can tell, for on her deck no

sailor has ever been seen to run up colors or heard
to answer a hail. Be it in calm or storm, in-come or
ebb of tide, the ship holds her way until she almost
touches shore.

There is no creak of spars or whine of cordage,
no spray at the bow, no ripple at the stern—no
voice, and no figure to utter one. As she nears the
rocks she pauses, then, as if impelled by a contrary
current, floats rudder foremost off to sea, and vanishes
in twilight. Harpswell is her favorite cruising-
ground, and her appearance there sets many heads
to shaking, for while it is not inevitable that ill luck
follows her visits, it has been seen that burial-boats
have sometimes had occasion to cross the harbor
soon after them, and that they were obliged by wind
or tide or current to follow her course on leaving
the wharf.

THE SCHOOLMASTER HAD NOT
REACHED ORRINGTON.

THE quiet town of Orrington, in Maine, was
founded by Jesse Atwood, of Wellfleet,
Cape Cod, in 1778, and has become known, since
then, as a place where skilful farmers and brave
sailors could always be found. It also kept Maine
supplied for years with oldest inhabitants. It is
said that the name was an accident of illiteracy, and
that it is the only place in the world that owes its
title to bad spelling. The settlers who followed

Myths and Legends

Atwood there were numerous enough to form a township after ten years, and the name they decided on for their commonwealth was Orangetown, so called for a village in Maryland where some of the people had associations, but the clerk of the town-meeting was not a college graduate and his spelling of Orange was Orring, and of town, ton. His draft of the resolutions went before the legislature, and the people directly afterward found themselves living in Orrington.

JACK WELCH'S DEATH LIGHT

POND COVE, Maine, is haunted by a light that on a certain evening, every summer, rises a mile out at sea, drifts to a spot on shore, then whirls with a buzz and a glare to an old house, where it vanishes. Its first appearance was simultaneous with the departure of Jack Welch, a fisherman. He was seen one evening at work on his boat, but in the morning he was gone, nor has he since shown himself in the flesh.

On the tenth anniversary of this event three fishermen were hurrying up the bay, hoping to reach home before dark, for they dreaded that uncanny light, but a fog came in and it was late before they reached the wharf. As they were tying their boat a channel seemed to open through the mist, and along that path from the deep came a ball of pallid flame with the rush of a meteor. There was one of the men who cowered at the bottom of the boat with ashen face and shaking limbs, and did not watch the light, even though it shot above his head, played through the rigging, and after a wide sweep went shoreward and settled on his house. Next day one of his comrades called for him, but Tom Wright was gone,— gone, his wife said, before the day broke. Like Jack Welch's disappearance, this departure was unexplained, and in time he was given up for dead.

Twenty years had passed, when Wright's presumptive widow was startled by the receipt of a letter in a weak, trembling hand, signed with her husband's name. It was written on his death-bed, in a distant place, and held a confession. Before their marriage, Jack Welch had been a suitor for her hand, and had been the favored of the two. To remove his rival and prosper in his place, Wright stole upon the other at his work, killed him, took his body to sea, and threw it overboard. Since that time the dead man had pursued him, and he was glad that the end of his days was come. But, though Tom Wright is no more, his victim's light comes yearly from the sea, above the spot where his body sank, floats to the scene of the murder on the shore, then flits to the house where the assassin lived and for years simulated the content that comes of wedded life.

Myths and Legends

MOGG MEGONE

HAPLESS daughter of a renegade is Ruth Bonython. Her father is as unfair to his friends as to his enemies, but to neither of them so merciless as to Ruth. Although he knows that she loves Master Scammon—in spite of his desertion—and would rather die than wed another, he has promised her to Mogg Megone, the chief who rules the Indians at the Saco mouth. He, blundering savage, fancies that he sees to the bottom of her grief, and one day, while urging his suit, he opens his blanket and shows the scalp of Scammon, to prove that he has avenged her. She looks in horror, but when he flings the bloody trophy at her feet she baptizes it with a forgiving tear. What villany may this lead to? Ah, none for him, for Bonython now steps in and plies him with flattery and drink, gaining from the chief, at last, his signature—the bow totem—to a transfer of the land for which he is willing to sell his daughter. Ruth, maddened at her father's meanness and the Indian's brutality, rushes on the imbruted savage, grasps from his belt the knife that has slain her lover, cleaves his heart in twain, and flies into the wood, leaving Bonython stupid with amazement.

Father Rasles, in his chapel at Norridgewock, is affecting his Indian converts against the Puritans, who settled to the southward of him fifty years before. To him comes a woman with torn garments and frightened face. Her dead mother stood before her last night, she says, and looked at her reprovingly, for she had killed Mogg Megone. The priest starts back in wrath, for Mogg was a hopeful agent of the faith, and bids her go, for she can ask no pardon. Brooding within his chapel, then, he is startled by the sound of shot and hum of arrows. Harmon and Moulton are advancing with their men and crying, " Down with the beast of Rome ! Death to the Babylonish dog !" Ruth, knowing not what this new misfortune may mean, runs from the church and disappears.

Some days later, old Baron Castine, going to Norridgewock to bury and revenge the dead, finds a woman seated on the earth and gazing over a field strewn with ashes and with human bones. He touches her. She is cold. There has been no life for days. It is Ruth.

THE LADY URSULA

IN 1690 a stately house stood in Kittery, Maine, a strongly guarded place with moat and draw-bridge (which was raised at night) and a moated grange adjacent where were cattle, sheep, and horses. Here, in lonely dignity, lived Lady Ur-sula, daughter of the lord of Grondale Abbey, across the water, whose distant grandeurs were in some sort reflected in this manor of the wilderness. Sil-ver, mahogany, paintings, tapestries, waxed floors,

Myths and Legends

and carven chests of linen represented wealth; prayers were said by a chaplain every morning and evening in the chapel, and, though the main hall would accommodate five hundred people, the lady usually sat at meat there with her thirty servants, her part of the table being raised two feet above theirs.

It was her happiness to believe that Captain Fowler, now absent in conflict with the French, would return and wed her according to his promise, but one day came a tattered messenger with bitter news of the captain's death. She made no talk of her grief, and, while her face was pale and step no longer light, she continued in the work that custom exacted from women of that time: help for the sick, alms for the poor, teaching for the ignorant, religion for the savage. Great was her joy, then, when a ship came from England bringing a letter from Captain Fowler himself, refuting the rumor of defeat and telling of his coming. Now the hall took on new life, reflecting the pleasure of its mistress; color came back to her cheek and sparkle to her eye, and she could only control her impatience by more active work and more aggressive charities. The day was near at hand for the arrival of her lover, when Ursula and her servants were set upon by Indians, while away from the protection of the manor, and slain. They were buried where they fell, and Captain Fowler found none to whom his love or sorrow could be told.

Tales of Puritan Land

FATHER MOODY'S BLACK VEIL

IN 1770 the Reverend Joseph Moody died at York, Maine, where he had long held the pastorate of a church, and where in his later years his face was never seen by friend or relative. At home, when any one was by, on the street, and in the pulpit his visage was concealed by a double fold of crape that was knotted above his forehead and fell to his chin, the lower edge of it being shaken by his breath. When first he presented himself to his congregation with features masked in black, great was the wonder and long the talk about it. Was he demented? His sermons were too logical for that. Had he been crossed in love? He could smile, though the smile was sad. Had he been scarred by accident or illness? If so, no physician knew of it.

After a time it was given out that his eyes were weakened by reading and writing at night, and the wonder ceased, though the veiled parson was less in demand for weddings, christenings, and social gatherings, and more besought for funerals than he had been. If asked to take off his crape he only replied, "We all wear veils of one kind or another, and the heaviest and darkest are those that hang about our hearts. This is but a material veil. Let it stay until the hour strikes when all faces shall be seen and all souls reveal their secrets."

Little by little the clergyman felt himself enforced

197

to withdraw from the public gaze. There were rough people who were impertinent and timid people who turned out of their road to avoid him, so that he found his out-door walks and meditations almost confined to the night, unless he chose the grave-yard for its seclusion or strolled on the beach and listened to the wallowing and grunting of the Black Boars— the rocks off shore that had laughed on the night when the York witch went up the chimney in a gale. But his life was long and kind and useful, and when at last the veiled head lay on the pillow it was never to rise from consciously, a fellow-clergyman came to soothe his dying moments and commend his soul to mercy.

To him, one evening, Father Moody said, " Brother, my hour is come and the veil of eternal darkness is falling over my eyes. Men have asked me why I wear this piece of crape about my face, as if it were not for them a reminder and a symbol, and I have borne the reason so long within me that only now have I resolved to tell it. Do you recall the finding of young Clark beside the river, years ago? He had been shot through the head. The man who killed him did so by accident, for he was a bosom friend ; yet he could never bring himself to confess the fact, for he dreaded the blame of his townsmen, the anguish of the dead man's parents, the hate of his betrothed. It was believed that the killing was a murder, and that some roving Indian had done it. After years of conscience-darkened life, in which the face of his dead friend often arose accusingly before him, the unhappy wretch vowed that he would never again look his fellows openly in the face: he would pay a penalty and conceal his shame. Then it was that I put a veil between myself and the world."

Joseph Moody passed away and, as he wished, the veil still hid his face in the coffin, but the clergyman who had raised it for a moment to compose his features, found there a serenity and a beauty that were majestic.

THE HOME OF THUNDER

SOME Indians believe that the Thunder Bird is the agent of storm; that the flashes of his eyes cause lightning and the flapping of his cloud-vast wings make thunder. Not so the Passamaquoddies, for they hold that Katahdin's spirit children are Thunders, and in this way an Indian found them: He had been seeking game along the Penobscot and for weeks had not met one of his fellow creatures. On a winter day he came on the print of a pair of snow-shoes; next morning the tracks appeared in another part of the forest, and so for many days he found them.

After a time it occurred to him to see where these tracks went to, and he followed them until they merged with others in a travelled road, ending at a precipice on the side of Katahdin (Great Mountain).

Myths and Legends

While lost in wonder that so many tracks should lead nowhere, he was roused by a footfall, and a maiden stepped from the precipice to the ledge beside him. Though he said nothing, being in awe of her stateliness and beauty, she replied in kind words to every unspoken thought and bade him go with her. He approached the rock with fear, but at a touch from the woman it became as mist, and they entered it together.

Presently they were in a great cave in the heart of Katahdin, where sat the spirit of the mountain, who welcomed them and asked the girl if her brothers had come. "I hear them coming," she replied. A blinding flash, a roar of thunder, and there stepped into the cave two men of giant size and gravely beautiful faces, hardened at the cheeks and brows to stone. "These," said the girl to the hunter, "are my brothers, the Thunder and the Lightning. My father sends them forth whenever there is wrong to redress, that those who love us may not be smitten. When you hear Thunder, know that they are shooting at our enemies."

At the end of that day the hunter returned to his home, and behold, he had been gone seven years. Another legend says that the stone-faced sons of the mountain adopted him, and that for seven years he was a roaming Thunder, but at the end of that time while a storm was raging he was allowed to fall, unharmed, into his own village.

Tales of Puritan Land

THE PARTRIDGE WITCH

TWO brothers, having hunted at the head of the Penobscot until their snow-shoes and moccasins gave out, looked at each other ruefully and cried, " Would that there was a woman to help us !" The younger brother went to the lodge that evening earlier than the elder, in order to prepare the supper, and great was his surprise on entering the wigwam to find the floor swept, a fire built, a pot boiling, and their clothing mended. Returning to the wood he watched the place from a covert until he saw a graceful girl enter the lodge and take up the tasks of housekeeping.

When he entered she was confused, but he treated her with respect, and allowed her to have her own way so far as possible, so that they became warm friends, sporting together like children when the work of the day was over. But one evening she said, " Your brother is coming. I fear him. Farewell." And she slipped into the wood. When the young man told his elder brother what had happened there—the elder having been detained for a few days in the pursuit of a deer—he declared that he would wish the woman to come back, and presently, without any summons, she returned, bringing a toboggan-load of garments and arms. The luck of the hunters improved, and they remained happily together until spring, when it was time to return with their furs.

Myths and Legends

They set off down the Penobscot in their canoe and rowed merrily along, but as they neared the home village the girl became uneasy, and presently "threw out her soul"—became clairvoyant—and said, "Let me land here. I find that your father would not like me, so do not speak to him about me." But the elder brother told of her when they reached home, whereon the father exclaimed, "I had feared this. That woman is a sister of the goblins. She wishes to destroy men."

At this the elder brother was afraid, lest she should cast a spell on him, and rowing up the river for a distance he came upon her as she was bathing and shot at her. The arrow seemed to strike, for there was a flutter of feathers and the woman flew away as a partridge. But the younger did not forget the good she had done and sought her in the wood, where for many days they played together as of old. "I do not blame your father: it is an affair of old, this hate he bears me," she said. "He will choose a wife for you soon, but do not marry her, else all will come to an end for you." The man could not wed the witch, and he might not disobey his father, in spite of this adjuration; so when the old man said to him, "I have a wife for you, my son," he answered, "It is well."

They brought the bride to the village, and for four days the wedding-dance was held, with a feast that lasted four days more. Then said the young man, "Now comes the end," and lying down on a bearskin he sighed a few times and his spirit ascended to the Ghosts' road—the milky way. The father shook his head, for he knew that this was the witch's work, and, liking the place no longer, he went away and the tribe was scattered.

THE MARRIAGE OF MOUNT KATAHDIN

AN Indian girl gathering berries on the side of Mount Katahdin looked up at its peak, rosy in the afternoon light, and sighed, "I wish that I had a husband. If Katahdin were a man he might marry me." Her companions laughed at this quaint conceit, and, filled with confusion at being overheard, she climbed higher up the slope and was lost to sight. For three years her tribe lost sight of her; then she came back with a child in her arms: a beautiful boy with brows of stone. The boy had wonderful power: he had only to point at a moose or a duck or a bear, and it fell dead, so that the tribe never wanted food. For he was the son of the Indian girl and the spirit of the mountain, who had commanded her not to reveal the boy's paternity. Through years she held silence on this point, holding in contempt, like other Indians, the prying inquiries of gossips and the teasing of young people, and knowing that Katahdin had designed the child for the founder of a mighty race, with the sinews of the very mountains in its frame, that should fill and rule the earth. Yet, one day, in anger at some slight, the mother spoke: " Fools ! Wasps who sting the fingers that pick you from the water ! Why do you torment me about what you might all see ? Look at the boy's face—his brows : in them do you not see Katahdin ? Now you have brought the curse upon yourselves, for you shall hunt your own venison from this time forth." Leading the child by the hand she turned toward the mountain and went out from their sight. And since then the Indians who could not hold their tongues, and who might otherwise have been great, have dwindled to a little people.

THE MOOSE OF MOUNT KINEO

EASTERN traditions concerning Hiawatha differ in many respects from those of the West. In the East he is known as Glooskap, god of the Passamaquoddies, and his marks are left in many places in the maritime provinces and Maine. It was he who gave names to things, created men, filled them with life, and moved their wonder with storms. He lived on the rocky height of Blomidon, at the entrance to Minas Basin, Nova Scotia, and the agates to be found along its foot are jewels that he made for his grandmother's necklace, when he restored her youth. He threw up a ridge between Fort Cumberland and Parrsboro, Nova Scotia, that he might cross, dry shod, the lake made by the beavers when they dammed the strait at Blomidon, but he afterward killed the beavers, and breaking down their dam he let the lake flow into the sea, and went southward on a hunting tour. At Mount Desert he killed a moose, whose bones he flung to the ground at Bar Harbor, where they are still to be seen, turned to stone, while across the bay he threw the entrails, and they, too, are visible as rocks, dented with his arrow-points. Mount Kineo was anciently a cow moose of colossal size that he slew and turned into a height of land, and the Indians trace the outline of the creature in the uplift to this day. Little Kineo was a calf moose that he slew at the same time, and Kettle Mountain is his camp-caldron that he flung to the ground in the ardor of the chase.

THE OWL TREE

ONE day in October, 1827, Rev. Charles Sharply rode into Alfred, Maine, and held service in the meeting-house. After the sermon he announced that he was going to Waterborough to preach, and that on his circuit he had collected two hundred and seventy dollars to help build a church in that village. Would not his hearers add to that sum? They would and did, and that evening the parson rode away with over three hundred dollars in his saddle-bags. He never appeared in Waterborough. Some of the country people gave tongue to their fear that the possession of the money had made him forget his sacred calling and that he had fled the State.

Myths and Legends

On the morning after his disappearance, however, Deacon Dickerman appeared in Alfred riding on a horse that was declared to be the minister's, until the tavern hostler affirmed that the minister's horse had a white star on forehead and breast, whereas this horse was all black. The deacon said that he found the horse grazing in his yard at daybreak, and that he would give it to whoever could prove it to be his property. Nobody appeared to demand it, and people soon forgot that it was not his. He extended his business at about that time and prospered; he became a rich man for a little place; though, as his wealth increased, he became morose and averse to company.

One day a rumor went around that a belated traveller had seen a misty thing under "the owl tree" at a turn of a road where owls were hooting, and that it took on a strange likeness to the missing clergyman. Dickerman paled when he heard this story, but he shook his head and muttered of the folly of listening to boy nonsense. Ten years had gone by—during that time the boys had avoided the owl tree after dark—when a clergyman of the neighborhood was hastily summoned to see Mr. Dickerman, who was said to be suffering from overwork. He found the deacon in his house alone, pacing the floor, his dress disordered, his cheek hectic.

"I have not long to live," said he, "nor would I live longer if I could. I am haunted day and night, and there is no peace, no rest for me on earth.

Tales of Puritan Land

They say that Sharply's spirit has appeared at the owl tree. Well, his body lies there. They accused me of taking his horse. It is true. A little black dye on his head and breast was all that was needed to deceive them. Pray for me, for I fear my soul is lost. I killed Sharply." The clergyman recoiled. "I killed him," the wretched man went on, "for the money that he had. The devil prospered me with it. In my will I leave two thousand dollars to his widow and five thousand dollars to the church he was collecting for. Will there be mercy for me there? I dare not think it. Go and pray for me." The clergyman hastened away, but was hardly outside the door when the report of a pistol brought him back. Dickerman lay dead on the floor. Sharply's body was exhumed from the shade of the owl tree, and the spot was never haunted after.

A CHESTNUT LOG

THERE is no doubt that farmer Lovel had read ancient history or he would not have been so ready in the emergency that befell him one time in the last century. He had settled among the New Hampshire hills near the site that is now occupied by the village of Washington and had a real good time there with bears and Indians. It was when he was splitting rails on Lovel Mountain—they named it for him afterward—that he found himself surrounded by six Indians, who told him that he was their prisoner. He agreed that they had the advantage over him and said that he would go quietly along if they would allow him to finish the big chestnut log that he was at work on. As he was a powerful fellow and was armed with an axe worth any two of their tomahawks, and as he would be pretty sure to have the life of at least one of them if they tried to drive him faster than he wanted to go, they consented. He said that he would be ready all the sooner if they would help him to pull the big log apart, and they agreed to help him. Driving a wedge into the long split he asked them to take hold, and when they had done this he knocked out the wedge with a single blow and the twelve hands were caught tight in the closing wood. Struggle as the savages might, they could not get free, and after calmly enjoying the situation for a few minutes he walked slowly from one to the other and split open the heads of all six. Then he went to work again splitting up more chestnuts.

THE WATCHER ON WHITE ISLAND

THE Isles of Shoals, a little archipelago of wind- and wave-swept rocks that may be seen on clear days from the New Hampshire coast, have been the scene of some mishaps and some crimes. On Boone Island, where the Nottingham galley went down one hundred and fifty years ago, the survivors turned cannibals to escape starvation, while

Tales of Puritan Land

Haley's Island is peopled by shipwrecked Spanish ghosts that hail vessels and beg for passage back to their country. The pirate Teach, or Blackbeard, used to put in at these islands to hide his treasure, and one of his lieutenants spent some time on White Island with a beautiful girl whom he had abducted from her home in Scotland and who, in spite of his rough life, had learned to love him. It was while walking with her on this rock, forgetful of his trade and the crimes he had been stained with, that one of his men ran up to report a sail that was standing toward the islands. The pirate ship was quickly prepared for action, but before embarking, mindful of possible flight or captivity, the lieutenant made his mistress swear that she would guard the buried treasure if it should be till doomsday.

The ship he was hurrying to meet came smoothly on until the pirate craft was well in range, when ports flew open along the stranger's sides, guns were run out, and a heavy broadside splintered through the planks of the robber galley. It was a man-of-war, not a merchantman, that had run Blackbeard down. The war-ship closed and grappled with the corsair, but while the sailors were standing at the chains ready to leap aboard and complete the subjugation of the outlaws a mass of flame burst from the pirate ship, both vessels were hurled in fragments through the air, and a roar went for miles along the sea. Blackbeard's lieutenant had fired the magazine rather than submit to capture, and had

blown the two ships into a common ruin. A few
of both crews floated to the islands on planks, sore
from burns and bruises, but none survived the cold
and hunger of the winter. The pirate's mistress
was among the first to die ; still, true to her promise,
she keeps her watch, and at night is dimly seen on
a rocky point gazing toward the east, her tall figure
enveloped in a cloak, her golden hair unbound upon
her shoulders, her pale face still as marble.

CHOCORUA

THIS beautiful alp in the White Mountains
commemorates in its name a prophet of the
Pequawket tribe who, prior to undertaking a journey,
had confided his son to a friendly settler, Cornelius
Campbell, of Tamworth. The boy found some
poison in the house that had been prepared for foxes,
and, thinking it to be some delicacy, he drank of it
and died. When Chocorua returned he could not
be persuaded that his son had fallen victim to his
own ignorance, but ascribed his death to the white
man's treachery, and one day, when Campbell entered his cabin from the fields, he found there
the corpses of his wife and children scalped and
mangled.

He was not a man to lament at such a time : hate
was stronger than sorrow. A fresh trail led from
his door. Seizing his rifle he set forth in pursuit
of the murderer. A mark in the dust, a bent grass

Tales of Puritan Land

blade, a torn leaf—these were guides enough, and following on through bush and swamp and wood they led him to this mountain, and up the slope he scrambled breathlessly. At the summit, statue-like, Chocorua stood. He saw the avenger coming, and knew himself unarmed, but he made no attempt to escape his doom. Drawing himself erect and stretching forth his hands he invoked anathema on his enemies in these words: "A curse upon you, white men! May the Great Spirit curse you when he speaks in the clouds, and his words are fire! Chocorua had a son and you killed him while the sky looked bright. Lightning blast your crops! Winds and fire destroy your dwellings! The Evil One breathe death upon your cattle! Your graves lie in the war-path of the Indian! Panthers howl and wolves fatten over your bones! Chocorua goes to the Great Spirit. His curse stays with the white man."

The report of Campbell's rifle echoed from the ledges and Chocorua leaped into the air, plunging to the rocks below. His mangled remains were afterward found and buried near the Tamworth path. The curse had its effect, for pestilence and storm devastated the surrounding country and the smaller settlements were abandoned. Campbell became a morose hermit, and was found dead in his bed two years afterward.

Myths and Legends

PASSACONAWAY'S RIDE TO HEAVEN

THE personality of Passaconaway, the powerful chief and prophet, is involved in doubt, but there can be no misprision of his wisdom. By some historians he has been made one with St. Aspenquid, the earliest of native missionaries among the Indians, who, after his conversion by French Jesuits, travelled from Maine to the Pacific, preaching to sixty-six tribes, healing the sick and working miracles, returning to die at the age of ninety-four. He was buried on the top of Agamenticus, Maine, where his manes were pacified with offerings of three thousand slain animals, and where his tombstone stood for a century after, bearing the legend, " Present, useful; absent, wanted; living, desired; dying, lamented."

By others Passaconaway is regarded as a different person. The Child of the Bear—to English his name—was the chief of the Merrimacs and a convert of the apostle Eliot. Natives and colonists alike admired him for his eloquence, his bravery, and his virtue. Before his conversion he was a reputed wizard who sought by magic arts to repel the invasion of his woods and mountains by the white men, invoking the spirits of nature against them from the topmost peak of the Agiochooks, and his native followers declared that in pursuance of this intent he made water burn, rocks move, trees dance, and transformed himself into a mass of flame.

Tales of Puritan Land

Such was his power over the forces of the earth that he could burn a tree in winter and from its ashes bring green leaves; he made dead wood blossom and a farmer's flail to bud, while a snake's skin he could cause to run. At the age of one hundred and twenty he retired from his tribe and lived in a lonely wigwam among the Pennacooks. One winter night the howling of wolves was heard, and a pack came dashing through the village harnessed by threes to a sledge of hickory saplings that bore a tall throne spread with furs. The wolves paused at Passaconaway's door. The old chief came forth, climbed upon the sledge, and was borne away with a triumphal apostrophe that sounded above the yelping and snarling of his train. Across Winnepesaukee's frozen surface they sped like the wind, and the belated hunter shrank aside as he saw the giant towering against the northern lights and heard his death-song echo from the cliffs. Through pathless woods, across ravines, the wolves sped on, with never slackened speed, into the mazes of the Agiochooks to that highest peak we now call Washington. Up its steep wilderness of snow the ride went furiously; the summit was neared, the sledge burst into flame, still there was no pause; the height was gained, the wolves went howling into darkness, but the car, wrapped in sheaves of fire, shot like a meteor toward the sky and was lost amid the stars of the winter night. So passed the Indian king to heaven.

Myths and Legends

THE BALL GAME BY THE SACO

WATER-GOBLINS from the streams about Katahdin had left their birthplace and journeyed away to the Agiochooks, making their presence known to the Indians of that region by thefts and loss of life. When the manitou, Glooskap, learned that these goblins were eating human flesh and committing other outrages, he took on their own form, turning half his body into stone, and went in search of them. The wigwam had been pitched near the Home of the Water Fairies,—a name absurdly changed by the people of North Conway to Diana's Bath,—and on entering he was invited to take meat. The tail of a whale was cooked and offered to him, but after he had taken it upon his knees one of the goblins exclaimed, " That is too good for a beggar like you," and snatched it away. Glooskap had merely to wish the return of the dainty when it flew back into his platter. Then he took the whale's jaw, and snapped it like a reed ; he filled his pipe and burned the tobacco to ashes in one inhalation ; when his hosts closed the wigwam and smoked vigorously, intending to foul the air and stupefy him, he enjoyed it, while they grew sick ; so they whispered to each other, " This is a mighty magician, and we must try his powers in another way."

A game of ball was proposed, and, adjourning to a sandy level at the bend of the Saco, they began to

play, but Glooskap found that the ball was a hideous
skull that rolled and snapped at him and would have
torn his flesh had it not been immortal and im-
movable from his bones.   He crushed it at a blow,
and breaking off the bough of a tree he turned it
by a word into a skull ten times larger than the
other that flew after the wicked people as a wildcat
leaps upon a rabbit.   Then the god stamped on the
sands and all the springs were opened in the mountains, so that the Saco came rising through the valley with a roar that made the nations tremble.   The
goblins were caught in the flood and swept into the
sea, where Glooskap changed them into fish.

THE WHITE MOUNTAINS

FROM times of old these noble hills have been
the scenes of supernatural visitations and
mysterious occurrences.   The tallest peak of the
Agiochooks—as they were, in Indian naming—was
the seat of God himself, and the encroachment
there of the white man was little liked.   Near
Fabyan's was once a mound, since levelled by pick
and spade, that was known as the Giant's Grave.
Ethan Allen Crawford, a skilful hunter, daring
explorer, and man of herculean frame, lived, died,
and is buried here, and near the ancient hillock he
built one of the first public houses in the mountains.
It was burned.   Another, and yet another hostelry
was builded on the site, but they likewise were

destroyed by fire. Then the enterprise was abandoned, for it was remembered that an Indian once mounted this grave, waved a torch from its top, and cried in a loud voice, " No pale-face shall take root on this spot. This has the Great Spirit whispered in my ear."

Governor Wentworth, while on a lonely tour through his province, found this cabin of Crawford's and passed a night there, tendering many compliments to the austere graces of the lady of the house and drinking himself into the favor of the husband, who proclaimed him the prince of good fellows. On leaving, the guest exacted of Crawford a visit to Wolfeborough, where he was to inquire for " Old Wentworth." This visit was undertaken soon after, and the sturdy frontiersman was dismayed at finding himself in the house of the royal governor ; but his reception was hearty enough to put him at his ease, and when he returned to the mountains he carried in his pocket a deed of a thousand acres of forest about his little farm. The family that he founded became wealthy and increased, by many an acre, the measure of that royal grant.

Not far below this spot, in the wildest part of the Notch, shut in by walls of rock thousands of feet high, is the old Willey House, and this, too, was the scene of a tragedy, for in 1826 a storm loosened the soil on Mount Willey and an enormous landslide occurred. The people in the house rushed forth on hearing the approach of the slide and met death almost at their door. Had they remained within they would have been unharmed, for the avalanche was divided by a wedge of rock behind the house, and the little inn was saved. Seven people are known to have been killed, and it was rumored that there was another victim in a young man whose name was unknown and who was walking through the mountains to enjoy their beauty. The messenger who bore the tidings of the destruction of the family was barred from reaching North Conway by the flood in the Saco, so he stood at the brink of the foaming river and rang a peal on a trumpet. This blast echoing around the hills in the middle of the night roused several men from their beds to know its meaning. The dog belonging to the inn is said to have given first notice to people below the Notch that something was wrong, but his moaning and barking were misunderstood, and after running back and forth, as if to summon help, he disappeared. At the hour of the accident James Willey, of Conway, had a dream in which he saw his dead brother standing by him. He related the story of the catastrophe to the sleeping man and said that when "the world's last knell" sounded they were going for safety to the foot of the steep mountain, for the Saco had risen twenty-four feet in seven hours and threatened to ingulf them in front.

Another spot of interest in the Notch is Nancy's Brook. It was at the point where this stream comes foaming from Mount Nancy into the great ravine

Myths and Legends

that the girl whose name is given to it was found
frozen to death in a shroud of snow in the fall of
1788. She had set out alone from Jefferson in search
of a young farmer who was to have married her, and
walked thirty miles through trackless snow between
sunset and dawn. Then her strength gave out and
she sank beside the road never to rise again. Her
recreant lover went mad with remorse when he
learned the manner of her death and did not long
survive her, and men who have traversed the savage
passes of the Notch on chill nights in October have
fancied that they heard, above the clash of the stream
and whispering of the woods, long, shuddering groans
mingled with despairing cries and gibbering laughter.

The birth of Peabody River came about from a
cataclysm of less violent nature than some of the
avalanches that have so scarred the mountains. In
White's "History of New England," Mr. Peabody,
for whom the stream is named, is reported as having
taken shelter in an Indian cabin on the heights
where the river has its source. During the night
a loud roaring waked the occupants of the hut and
they sprang forth, barely in time to save their lives;
for, hardly had they gained the open ground before
a cavern burst open in the hill and a flood of water
gushed out, sweeping away the shelter and cutting a
broad swath through the forest.

Although the Pilot Mountains are supposed to
have taken their name from the fact that they served
as landmarks to hunters who were seeking the Con-

218

necticut River from the Lancaster district, an old
story is still told of one Willard, who was lost amid
the defiles of this range, and nearly perished with
hunger. While lying exhausted on the mountain-
side his dog would leave him every now and then
and return after a couple of hours. Though Willard
was half dead, he determined to use his last strength
in following the animal, and as a result was led by
a short cut to his own camp, where provisions were
plenty, and where the intelligent creature had been
going for food. The dog was christened Pilot, in
honor of this service, and the whole range is thought
by many to be named in his honor.

Waternomee Falls, on Hurricane Creek, at War-
ren, are bordered with rich moss where fairies used
to dance and sing in the moonlight. These sprites
were the reputed children of Indians that had been
stolen from their wigwams and given to eat of fairy
bread, that dwarfed and changed them in a moment.
Barring their kidnapping practices the elves were an
innocent and joyous people, and they sought more
distant hiding-places in the wilderness when the stern
churchmen and cruel rangers penetrated their sylvan
precincts.

An old barrack story has it that John Chamberlain, who fought under Lovewell, was pursued
along the base of Melvin Peak by Indians and
was almost in their grasp when he reached Ossipee
Falls. It seemed as if there were no alternative between death by the tomahawk and death by a fall to

the rocks below, for the chasm here is eighteen feet wide; but without stopping to reckon chances he put his strength into a running jump, and to the amazement of those in pursuit and perhaps to his own surprise he cleared the gap and escaped into the woods. The foremost of the Indians attempted the leap, but plunged to his death in the ravine.

The Eagle Range was said to be the abode, two hundred years ago, of a man of strange and venerable appearance, whom the Indians regarded with superstitious awe and never tried to molest. He slept in a cave on the south slope and ranged the forest in search of game, muttering and gesturing to himself. He is thought to be identified with Thomas Crager, whose wife had been hanged in Salem as a witch, and whose only child had been stolen by Indians. After a long, vain search for the little one he gave way to a bitter moroseness, and avoided the habitations of civilized man and savages alike. It is a satisfaction to know that before he died he found his daughter, though she was the squaw of an Indian hunter and was living with his tribe on the shore of the St. Lawrence.

THE VISION ON MOUNT ADAMS

THERE are many traditions connected with Mount Adams that have faded out of memory. Old people remember that in their childhood there was talk of the discovery of a magic stone;

Tales of Puritan Land

of an Indian's skeleton that appeared in a speaking storm; of a fortune-teller that set off on a midnight quest, far up among the crags and eyries. In October, 1765, a detachment of nine of Rogers's Rangers began the return from a Canadian foray, bearing with them plate, candlesticks, and a silver statue that they had rifled from the Church of St. Francis. An Indian who had undertaken to guide the party through the Notch proved faithless, and led them among labyrinthine gorges to the head of Israel's River, where he disappeared, after poisoning one of the troopers with a rattlesnake's fang. Losing all reckoning, the Rangers tramped hither and thither among the snowy hills and sank down, one by one, to die in the wilderness, a sole survivor reaching a settlement after many days, with his knapsack filled with human flesh.

In 1816 the candlesticks were recovered near Lake Memphremagog, but the statue has never been laid hold upon. The spirits of the famished men were wont, for many winters, to cry in the woods, and once a hunter, camped on the side of Mount Adams, was awakened at midnight by the notes of an organ. The mists were rolling off, and he found that he had gone to sleep near a mighty church of stone that shone in soft light. The doors were flung back, showing a tribe of Indians kneeling within. Candles sparkled on the altar, shooting their rays through clouds of incense, and the rocks shook with thunder-gusts of music. Suddenly church, lights, worshippers vanished, and from the mists came forth a line of uncouth forms, marching in silence. As they started to descend the mountain a silver image, floating in the air, spread a pair of gleaming pinions and took flight, disappearing in the chaos of battlemented rocks above.

THE GREAT CARBUNCLE

HIGH on the eastern face of Mount Monroe shone the Great Carbuncle, its flash scintillating for miles by day, its dusky crimson glowing among the ledges at night. The red men said that it hung in the air, and that the soul of an Indian—killed, that he might guard the spot—made approach perilous to men of all complexions and purposes. As late as Ethan Crawford's time one search band took a "good man" to lay the watcher, when they strove to scale the height, but they returned "sorely bruised, treasureless, and not even saw that wonderful sight." The value of the stone tempted many, but those who sought it had to toil through a dense forest, and on arriving at the mountain found its glories eclipsed by intervening abutments, nor could they get near it. Rocks covered with crystals, at first thought to be diamonds, were readily despoiled of their treasure, but the Great Carbuncle burned on, two thousand feet above them, at the head of the awful chasm of Oakes Gulf, and baffled seekers likened it to the glare of an evil eye.

Tales of Puritan Land

There was one who had grown old in searching for this gem, often scrambling over the range in wind and snow and cloud, and at last he reached a precipitous spot he had never attained before. Great was his joy, for the Carbuncle was within his reach, blazing into his eyes in the noon sunlight as if it held, crystallized in its depths, the brightness of all the wine that had ever gladdened the tired hearts of men. There were rivals in the search, and on reaching the plateau they looked up and saw him kneeling on a narrow ledge with arms extended as in rapture. They called to him. He answered not. He was dead—dead of joy and triumph. While they looked a portion of the crag above him fell away and rolled from rock to rock, marking its course with flashes of bloody fire, until it reached the Lake of the Clouds, and the waters of that tarn drowned its glory. Yet those waters are not always black, and sometimes the hooked crest of Mount Monroe is outlined against the night sky in a ruddy glow.

SKINNER'S CAVE

THE abhorrence to paying taxes and duties—or any other levy from which an immediate and personal good is not promised—is too deeply rooted in human nature to be affected by statutes, and whenever it is possible to buy commodities that have escaped the observation of the revenue officers many are tempted to do so for the mere pleasure of defying

Myths and Legends

the law.   In the early part of this century the northern farmers and their wives were, in a way, providing themselves with laces, silver-ware, brandy, and other protected and dreadful articles, on which it was evident that somebody had forgotten to pay duty. The customs authorities on the American side of the border were long puzzled by the irruption of these forbidden things, but suspicion ultimately fell on a fellow of gigantic size, named Skinner.

It was believed that this outlaw carried on the crime of free trade after sunset, hiding his merchandise by day on the islands of Lake Memphremagog. This delightful sheet of water lies half in Canada and half in Vermont—agreeably to the purpose of such as he.   Province Island is still believed to contain buried treasure, but the rock that contains Skinner's Cave was the smuggler's usual haunt, and when pursued he rowed to this spot and effected a disappearance, because he entered the cave on the northwest side, where it was masked by shrubbery.   One night the officers landed on this island after he had gone into hiding, and after diligent search discovered his boat drawn up in a covert.   They pushed it into the lake, where the winds sent it adrift, and, his communication with the shore thus cut off, the outlaw perished miserably of hunger.   His skeleton was found in the cavern some years later.

YET THEY CALL IT LOVER'S LEAP

IN the lower part of the township of Cavendish, Vermont, the Black River seeks a lower level through a gorge in the foot-hills of the Green Mountains. The scenery here is romantic and impressive, for the river makes its way along the ravine in a series of falls and rapids that are overhung by trees and ledges, while the geologist finds something worth looking at in the caves and pot-holes that indicate an older level of the river. At a turn in the ravine rises the sheer precipice of Lover's Leap. It is a vertical descent of about eighty feet, the water swirling at its foot in a black and angry maelstrom. It is a spot whence lovers might easily step into eternity, were they so disposed, and the name fits delightfully into the wild and somber scene; but ask any good villager thereabout to relate the legend of the place and he will tell you this:

About forty years ago a couple of young farmers went to the Leap—which then had no name—to pry out some blocks of the schistose rock for a foundation wall. They found a good exposure of the rock beneath the turf and began to quarry it. In the earnestness of the work one of the men forgot that he was standing on the verge of a precipice, and through a slip of his crowbar he lost his balance and went reeling into the gulf. His horrified companion crept to the edge, expecting to see his mangled corpse tossing in the whirlpool, but, to his amazement, the unfortunate was crawling up the face of a huge table of stone that had fallen from the opposite wall and lay canted against it.

" Hello !" shouted the man overhead. " Are you hurt much ?"

The victim of the accident slowly got upon his feet, felt cautiously of his legs and ribs, and began to search through his pockets, his face betraying an anxiety that grew deeper and deeper as the search went on. In due time the answer came back, deliberate, sad, and nasal, but distinct above the roar of the torrent: " Waal, I ain't hurt much, but I'll be durned if I haven't lost my jack-knife !"

And he was pulled out of the gorge without it.

SALEM AND OTHER WITCHCRAFT

THE extraordinary delusion recorded as Salem witchcraft was but a reflection of a kindred insanity in the Old World that was not extirpated until its victims had been counted by thousands. That human beings should be accused of leaguing themselves with Satan to plague their fellows and overthrow the powers of righteousness is remarkable, but that they should admit their guilt is incomprehensible, albeit the history of every popular delusion shows that weak minds are so affected as to lose control of themselves and that a whimsey can be as epidemic as small-pox.

Such was the case in 1692 when the witchcraft

madness, which might have been stayed by a season-
able spanking, broke out in Danvers, Massachusetts,
the first victim being a wild Irishwoman, named
Glover, and speedily involved the neighboring community of Salem. The mischiefs done by witches
were usually trifling, and it never occurred to their
prosecutors that there was an inconsistency between
their pretended powers and their feeble deeds, or
that it was strange that those who might live in regal
luxury should be so wretchedly poor. Aches and
pains, blight of crops, disease of cattle, were charged
to them ; children complained of being pricked with
thorns and pins (the pins are still preserved in Salem),
and if hysterical girls spoke the name of any feeble
old woman, while in flighty talk, they virtually sentenced her to die. The word of a child of eleven
years sufficed to hang a witch.

Giles Corey, a blameless man of eighty, was condemned to the mediæval *peine forte et dure*, his body
being crushed beneath a load of rocks and timbers.
He refused to plead in court, and when the beams
were laid upon him he only cried, " More weight !"
The shade of the unhappy victim haunted the scene
of his execution for years, and always came to warn
the people of calamities. A young child and a dog
were also hanged after formal condemnation. Gallows Hill, near Salem, witnessed many sad tragedies,
and the old elm that stood on Boston Common
until 1876 was said to have served as a gallows for
witches and Quakers. The accuser of one day was

the prisoner of the next, and not even the clergy were safe.

A few escapes were made, like that of a blue-eyed maid of Wenham, whose lover aided her to break the wooden jail and carried her safely beyond the Merrimac, finding a home for her among the Quakers; and that of Miss Wheeler, of Salem, who had fallen under suspicion, and whose brothers hurried her into a boat, rowed around Cape Ann, and safely bestowed her in "the witch house" at Pigeon Cove. Many, however, fled to other towns rather than run the risk of accusation, which commonly meant death.

When the wife of Philip English was arrested he, too, asked to share her fate, and both were, through friendly intercession, removed to Boston, where they were allowed to have their liberty by day on condition that they would go to jail every night. Just before they were to be taken back to Salem for trial they went to church and heard the Rev. Joshua Moody preach from the text, "If they persecute you in one city, flee unto another." The good clergyman not only preached goodness, but practised it, and that night the door of their prison was opened. Furnished with an introduction from Governor Phipps to Governor Fletcher, of New York, they made their way to that settlement, and remained there in safe and courteous keeping until the people of Salem had regained their senses, when they returned. Mrs. English died, soon after, from the effects of cruelty and anxiety, and although Mr. Moody was generally commended for his substitution of sense and justice for law, there were bigots who persecuted him so constantly that he removed to Plymouth.

According to the belief of the time a witch or wizard compacted with Satan for the gift of supernatural power, and in return was to give up his soul to the evil one after his life was over. The deed was signed in blood of the witch and horrible ceremonies confirmed the compact. Satan then gave his ally a familiar in the form of a dog, ape, cat, or other animal, usually small and black, and sometimes an undisguised imp. To suckle these "familiars" with the blood of a witch was forbidden in English law, which ranked it as a felony; but they were thus nourished in secret, and by their aid the witch might raise storms, blight crops, abort births, lame cattle, topple over houses, and cause pains, convulsions, and illness. If she desired to hurt a person she made a clay or waxen image in his likeness, and the harms and indignities wreaked on the puppet would be suffered by the one bewitched, a knife or needle thrust in the waxen body being felt acutely by the living one, no matter how far distant he might be. By placing this image in running water, hot sunshine, or near a fire, the living flesh would waste as this melted or dissolved, and the person thus wrought upon would die. This belief is still current among negroes affected by the voodoo super-

stition of the South. The witch, too, had the
power of riding winds, usually with a broomstick
for a conveyance, after she had smeared the broom
or herself with magic ointment, and the flocking of
the unhallowed to their sabbaths in snaky bogs or
on lonely mountain tops has been described minutely
by those who claim to have seen the sight. Sometimes they cackled and gibbered through the night
before the houses of the clergy, and it was only at
Christmas that their power failed them. The meetings were devoted to wild and obscene orgies, and
the intercourse of fiends and witches begot a progeny
of toads and snakes.

Naturally the Indians were accused, for they
recognized the existence of both good and evil
spirits, their medicine-men cured by incantations
in the belief that devils were thus driven out of
their patients, and in the early history of the country
the red man was credited by white settlers with
powers hardly inferior to those of the oriental and
European magicians of the middle ages. Cotton
Mather detected a relation between Satan and the
Indians, and he declares that certain of the Algon-
quins were trained from boyhood as powahs, powwows, or wizards, acquiring powers of second sight
and communion with gods and spirits through absti-
nence from food and sleep and the observance of rites.
Their severe discipline made them victims of nervous
excitement and the responsibilities of conjuration
had on their minds an effect similar to that produced

Tales of Puritan Land

by gases from the rift in Delphos on the Apollonian
oracles, their manifestations of insanity or frenzy
passing for deific or infernal possession. When
John Gibb, a Scotchman, who had gone mad through
religious excitement, was shipped to this country by
his tired fellow-countrymen, the Indians hailed him as
a more powerful wizard than any of their number, and
he died in 1720, admired and feared by them because
of the familiarity with spirits out of Hobbomocko
(hell) that his ravings and antics were supposed to
indicate. Two Indian servants of the Reverend Mr.
Parris, of Salem, having tried by a spell to discover
a witch, were executed as witches themselves. The
savages, who took Salem witchcraft at its worth,
were astonished at its deadly effect, and the English
may have lost some influence over the natives in
consequence of this madness. "The Great Spirit
sends no witches to the French," they said. Barrow
Hill, near Amesbury, was said to be the meeting-
place for Indian powwows and witches, and at late
hours of the night the light of fires gleamed from
its top, while shadowy forms glanced athwart it.
Old men say that the lights are still there in winter,
though modern doubters declare that they were the
aurora borealis.

But the belief in witches did not die even when
the Salem people came to their senses. In the
Merrimac valley the devil found converts for many
years after: Goody Mose, of Rocks village, who
tumbled down-stairs when a big beetle was killed at

an evening party, some miles away, after it had been
bumping into the faces of the company; Goody
Whitcher, of Amesbury, whose loom kept banging
day and night after she was dead; Goody Sloper,
of West Newbury, who went home lame directly
that a man had struck his axe into the beam of a
house that she had bewitched, but who recovered
her strength and established an improved reputation
when, in 1794, she swam out to a capsized boat and
rescued two of the people who were in peril;
Goodman Nichols, of Rocks village, who " spelled"
a neighbor's son, compelling him to run up one end
of the house, along the ridge, and down the other
end, " troubling the family extremely by his strange
proceedings;" Susie Martin, also of Rocks, who
was hanged in spite of her devotions in jail, though
the rope danced so that it could not be tied, but a
crow overhead called for a withe and the law was
executed with that; and Goody Morse, of Market
and High Streets, Newburyport, whose baskets and
pots danced through her house continually and who
was seen " flying about the sun as if she had been
cut in twain, or as if the devil did hide the lower
part of her." The hill below Easton, Pennsylvania,
called Hexenkopf (Witch's head), was described by
German settlers as a place of nightly gathering for
weird women, who whirled about its top in " linked
dances" and sang in deep tones mingled with awful
laughter. After one of these women, in Williams
township, had been punished for enchanting a

Tales of Puritan Land

twenty-dollar horse, their sabbaths were held more quietly. Mom Rinkle, whose "rock" is pointed out beside the Wissahickon, in Philadelphia, "drank dew from acorn-cups and had the evil eye." Juan Perea, of San Mateo, New Mexico, would fly with his chums to meetings in the mountains in the shape of a fire-ball. During these sallies he left his own eyes at home and wore those of some brute animal. It was because his dog ate his eyes when he had carelessly put them on a table that he had always afterward to wear those of a cat. Within the present century an old woman who lived in a hut on the Palisades of the Hudson was held to be responsible for local storms and accidents. As late as 1889 two Zuñi Indians were hanged on the wall of an old Spanish church near their pueblo in Arizona on a charge of having blown away the rain-clouds in a time of drouth. It was held that there was something uncanny in the event that gave the name of Gallows Hill to an eminence near Falls Village, Connecticut, for a strange black man was found hanging, dead, to a tree near its top one morning.

Moll Pitcher, a successful sorcerer and fortune-teller of old Lynn, has figured in obsolete poems, plays, and romances. She lived in a cottage at the foot of High Rock, where she was consulted, not merely by people of respectability, but by those who had knavish schemes to prosecute and who wanted to learn in advance the outcome of their

designs. Many a ship was deserted at the hour of
sailing because she boded evil of the voyage. She
was of medium height, big-headed, tangle-haired,
long-nosed, and had a searching black eye. The
sticks that she carried were cut from a hazel that
hung athwart a brook where an unwedded mother
had drowned her child. A girl who went to her
for news of her lover lost her reason when the witch,
moved by a malignant impulse, described his death
in a fiercely dramatic manner. One day the missing
ship came bowling into port, and the shock of joy
that the girl experienced when the sailor clasped
her in his arms restored her erring senses. When
Moll Pitcher died she was attended by the little
daughter of the woman she had so afflicted.

John, or Edward, Dimond, grandfather of Moll
Pitcher, was a benevolent wizard. When vessels
were trying to enter the port of Marblehead in a
heavy gale or at night, their crews were startled to
hear a trumpet voice pealing from the skies, plainly
audible above the howling and hissing of any tempest, telling them how to lay their course so as to
reach smooth water. This was the voice of Dimond,
speaking from his station, miles away in the village
cemetery. He always repaired to this place in
troublous weather and shouted orders to the ships
that were made visible to him by mystic power as
he strode to and fro among the graves. When
thieves came to him for advice he charmed them and
made them take back their plunder or caused them

to tramp helplessly about the streets bearing heavy burdens.

> " Old Mammy Redd, of Marblehead,
> Sweet milk could turn to mould in churn."

Being a witch, and a notorious one, she could likewise curdle the milk as it came from the cow, and afterward transform it into blue wool. She had the evil eye, and, if she willed, her glance or touch could blight like palsy. It only needed that she should wish a bloody cleaver to be found in a cradle to cause the little occupant to die, while the whole town ascribed to her the annoyances of daily house-work and business. Her unpleasant celebrity led to her death at the hands of her fellow-citizens who had been " worrited" by no end of queer happen-ings : ships had appeared just before they were wrecked and had vanished while people looked at them ; men were seen walking on the water after they had been comfortably buried ; the wind was heard to name the sailors doomed never to return ; footsteps and voices were heard in the streets before the great were to die ; one man was chased by a corpse in its coffin ; another was pursued by the devil in a carriage drawn by four white horses ; a young woman who had just received a present of some fine fish from her lover was amazed to see him melt into the air, and was heart-broken when she learned next morning that he had died at sea. So far away as Amesbury the devil's power was shown by the appearance of a man who walked the roads carrying his head under his arm, and by the freak of a windmill that the miller always used to shut up at sundown but that started by itself at midnight. Evidently it was high time to be rid of Mammy Redd.

Margaret Wesson, "old Meg," lived in Gloucester until she came to her death by a shot fired at the siege of Louisburg, five hundred miles away, in 1745. Two soldiers of Gloucester, while before the walls of the French town, were annoyed by a crow, that flew over and around them, cawing harshly and disregarding stones and shot, until it occurred to them that the bird could be no other than old Meg in another form, and, as silver bullets are an esteemed antidote for the evils of witchcraft, they cut two silver buttons from their uniforms and fired them at the crow. At the first shot its leg was broken; at the second, it fell dead. On returning to Gloucester they learned that old Meg had fallen and broken her leg at the moment when the crow was fired on, and that she died quickly after. An examination of her body was made, and the identical buttons were extracted from her flesh that had been shot into the crow at Louisburg.

As a citizen of New Haven was riding home— this was at the time of the goings on at Salem—he saw shapes of women near his horse's head, whispering earnestly together and keeping time with the trot of his animal without effort of their own. "In the name of God, tell me who you are," cried the

traveller, and at the name of God they vanished.
Next day the man's orchard was shaken by viewless
hands and the fruit thrown down. Hogs ran about
the neighborhood on their hind legs; children cried
that somebody was sticking pins into them; one
man would roll across the floor as if pushed, and he
had to be watched lest he should go into the fire;
when housewives made their bread they found it as
full of hair as food in a city boarding-house; when
they made soft soap it ran from the kettle and over
the floor like lava; stones fell down chimneys and
smashed crockery. One of the farmers cut off an
ear from a pig that was walking on its hind legs, and
an eccentric old body of the neighborhood appeared
presently with one of her ears in a muffle, thus
satisfying that community that she had caused the
troubles. When a woman was making potash it
began to leap about, and a rifle was fired into the
pot, causing a sudden calm. In the morning the
witch was found dead on her floor. Yet killing
only made her worse, for she moved to a deserted
house near her own, and there kept a mad revel
every night; fiddles were heard, lights flashed,
stones were thrown, and yells gave people at a distance a series of cold shivers; but the populace tried
the effect of tearing down the house, and quiet was
brought to the town.

In the early days of this century a skinny old
woman known as Aunt Woodward lived by herself
in a log cabin at Minot Corner, Maine, enjoying

the awe of the people in that secluded burg. They moved around but little at night, on her account, and one poor girl was in mortal fear lest by mysterious arts she should be changed, between two days, into a white horse. One citizen kept her away from his house by nailing a horseshoe to his door, while another took the force out of her spells by keeping a branch of "round wood" at his threshold. At night she haunted a big, square house where the ghost of a murdered infant was often heard to cry, and by day she laid charms on her neighbors' provisions and utensils, and turned their cream to buttermilk. "Uncle" Blaisdell hurried into the settlement to tell the farmers that Aunt Woodward had climbed into his sled in the middle of the road, and that his four yoke of oxen could not stir it an inch, but that after she had leaped down one yoke of cattle drew the load of wood without an effort. Yet she died in her bed.

THE GLOUCESTER LEAGUERS

STRANGE things had been reported in Gloucester. On the eve of King Philip's War the march of men was heard in its streets and an Indian bow and scalp were seen on the face of the moon, while the boom of cannon and roll of drums were heard at Malden and the windows of Plymouth rattled to the passage of unseen horsemen. But the strangest thing was the arrival on Cape Ann of a

Tales of Puritan Land

force of French and Indians that never could be
caught, killed, or crippled, though two regiments
were hurried into Gloucester and battled with them
for a fortnight. Thus, the rumor went around that
these were not an enemy of flesh and blood, but
devils who hoped to work a moral perversion of the
colony. From 1692, when they appeared, until
Salem witchcraft was at an end, Cape Ann was
under military and spiritual guard against "the
spectre leaguers."

Another version of the episode, based on sworn
evidence, has it that Ebenezer Babson, returning
late on a summer night, saw two men run from his
door and vanish in a field. His family denied that
visitors had called, so he gave chase, for he believed
the men to have a mischievous intention. As he
left the threshold they sprang from behind a log,
one saying to the other, "The master of the house
is now come, else we might have taken the house,"
and again they disappeared in a swamp. Babson
woke the guard, and on entering the quarters of the
garrison the sound of many feet was heard without,
but when the doors were flung open only the two
men were visible and they were retreating. Next
evening the yeoman was chased by these elusive
gentry, who were believed to be scouts of the
enemy, for they wore white breeches and waist-
coats and carried bright guns.

For several nights they appeared, and on the 14th
of July half a dozen of them were seen so plainly

that the soldiers made a sally, Babson bringing three
of " ye unaccountable troublers" to the ground with
a single shot, and getting a response in kind, for a
bullet hissed by his ear and buried itself in a tree.
When the company approached the place where lay
the victims of that remarkable shot, behold, they
arose and scampered away as blithely as if naught
had happened to them. One of the trio was cor-
nered and shot anew, but when they would pick
him up he melted into air. There was fierce jab-
bering in an unknown tongue, through all the swamp,
and by the time the garrison had returned the fellows
were skulking in the shrubbery again. Richard
Dolliver afterward came on eleven of them engaged in
incantations and scattered them with a gunshot, but
they would not down. They lurked about the cape
until terror fell on all the people, remaining for
" the best part of a month together," so it was
deemed that " Satan had set ambushments against
the good people of Gloucester, with demons in the
shape of armed Indians and Frenchmen."

Stones were thrown, barns were beaten with
clubs, the marching of unseen hosts was heard after
dark, the mockers grew so bold that they ventured
close to the redoubtable Babson, gazed scornfully
down the barrel of his gun, and laid a charm on the
weapon, so that, no matter how often he snapped it
at them, it flashed in the pan. Neighboring garri-
sons were summoned, but all battling with goblins
was fruitless. One night a dark and hostile throng

emerged from the wood and moved toward the block-house, where twenty musketeers were keeping guard. "If you be ghosts or devils I will foil you," cried the captain, and tearing a silver button from his doublet he rammed it into his gun and fired on the advancing host. Even as the smoke of his musket was blown on the wind, so did the beleaguering army vanish, the silver bullet proving that they were not of human kind. The night was wearing on when a cry went out that the devils were coming again. Arms were laid aside this time, and the watchers sank to their knees in prayer. Directly that the name of God was uttered the marching ceased and heaven rang with the howls of the angry fiends. Never again were leaguers seen in Gloucester.

SATAN AND HIS BURIAL-PLACE

SATAN appears to have troubled the early settlers in America almost as grievously as he did the German students. He came in many shapes to many people, and sometimes he met his match. Did he not try to stop old Peter Stuyvesant from rowing through Hell Gate one moonlight night, and did not that tough old soldier put something at his shoulder that Satan thought must be his wooden leg? But it wasn't a leg: it was a gun, loaded with a silver bullet that had been charged home with prayer. Peter fired and the missile whistled off to Ward's Island,

where three boys found it afterward and swapped it
for double handfuls of doughnuts and bulls' eyes.
Incidentally it passed between the devil's ribs and
the fiend exploded with a yell and a smell, the latter
of sulphur, to Peter's blended satisfaction and alarm.
And did not the same spirit of evil plague the old
women of Massachusetts Bay and craze the French
and Spaniards in the South? At Hog Rock, west
of Milford, Connecticut, he broke up a pleasant
diversion :

> " Once four young men upon ye rock
>   Sate down at chuffle board to play
>   When ye Deuill appearde in shape of a hogg
>   And frightend ym so they scampered away
>   And left Old Nick to finish ye play."

One of the first buildings to be put up in Ipswich,
Massachusetts, was a church built on a ledge above
the river, and in that church Satan tried to conceal
himself for purposes of mischief. For this act he was
hurled from the steeple-top by some unseen instrument of righteousness with such force that his hoof-
mark was stamped into a solid stone near by. This
did not deter him from mounting to the ridge-pole
and assuming a defiant air, with folded arms, when
Whitefield began to preach, but when that clergyman's tremendous voice was loosed below him he
bounced into the air in terror and disappeared.

The Shakers report that in the waning of the
eighteenth century they chased the evil one through

Tales of Puritan Land

the coverts of Mount Sinai, Massachusetts, and just before dawn of a summer morning they caught and killed and buried him. Shakers are spiritualists, and they believe their numbers to have been augmented by distinguished dead, among whom they already number Washington, Lafayette, Napoleon, Tamerlane, and Pocahontas. The two first named of these posthumous communists are still seen by members of the faith who pass Satan's grave at night, for they sit astride of white horses and watch the burial spot, lest the enemy of man arise and begin anew his career of trouble. Some members of the brotherhood say that this legend typifies a burial of evil tendencies in the hearts of those who hunted the fiend, but it has passed down among others as a circumstance. The Shakers have many mystic records, transmitted verbally to the present disciples of " Mother Ann," but seldom told to scoffers " in the world," as those are called who live without their pure and peaceful communes. Among these records is that of the appearance of John the Baptist in the meeting-house at Mount Lebanon, New York, one Sunday, clothed in light and leading the sacred dance of the worshippers, by which they signify the shaking out of all carnal things from the heart.

Myths and Legends

PETER RUGG, THE MISSING MAN

THE idea of long wandering as a penalty, symbolized in "The Wandering Jew," "The Flying Dutchman," and the character of Kundry, in "Parsifal," has application in the legend of Peter Rugg. This strange man, who lived in Middle Street, Boston, with his wife and daughter, was esteemed as a person of probity and good manners except in his swearing fits, for he was subject to outbursts of passion, when he would kick his way through doors instead of opening them, bite ten-penny nails in two, and curse his wig off. In the autumn of 1770 he visited Concord, with his little girl, and on the way home was overtaken by a violent storm. He took shelter with a friend at Menotomy, who urged him to stay all night, for the rain was falling heavier every moment; but Rugg would not be stayed, and seeing that there was no hope of a dry journey back to town he roared a fearful oath and cried, "Let the storm increase. I will see home to-night in spite of it, or may I never see home!" With that he tossed the child into the open chaise, leaped in after her, lashed his horse, and was off.

Several nights afterward, while Rugg's neighbors were out with lanterns trying to discover the cause of a heavy jarring that had begun to disturb them in bad weather, the excitable gentleman, who had not been seen since his Concord visit, came whirling along the pavement in his carriage, his daughter beside him, his black horse plunging on in spite of his efforts to stop him. The lanterns that for a moment twinkled in Peter's face showed him as a wet and weary man, with eyes turned up longingly at the windows where his wife awaited him; then he was gone, and the ground trembled as with an earthquake, while the rain fell more heavily.

Mrs. Rugg died within a twelvemonth, and Peter never reached home, but from all parts of New England came stories of a man and child driving rapidly along the highways, never stopping except to inquire the way to Boston. Half of the time the man would be headed in a direction opposite to the one he seemed to want to follow, and when set right would cry that he was being deceived, and was sometimes heard to mutter, "No home to-night." In Hartford, Providence, Newburyport, and among the New Hampshire hills the anxious face of the man became known, and he was referred to as "the storm-breeder," for so surely as he passed there would be rain, wind, lightning, thunder, and darkness within the hour.

Some years ago a man in a Connecticut town stopped this hurrying traveller, who said, in reply to a question, "I have lost the road to Boston. My name is Peter Rugg." Then Rugg's disappearance half a century before was cited by those who had long memories, and people began to look askant at Peter and gave him generous road room when they met him. The toll-taker on Charlestown bridge declared that he had been annoyed and alarmed by a prodigious tramping of hoofs and rattling of wheels that seemed to pass toward Boston before his very face, yet he could see nothing. He took courage one night to plant himself in the middle of the bridge with a three-legged stool, and when the sound approached he dimly saw a large black horse driven by a weary looking man with a child beside him. The stool was flung at the horse's head, but passed through the animal as through smoke and skipped across the floor of the bridge. Thus much the toll-collector said, but when asked if Rugg had appeared again he made no reply.

THE LOSS OF WEETAMOO

WINNEPURKIT, sagamore of the coast settlements between Nahant and Cape Ann, had married Weetamoo, daughter of Passaconaway, king of the Pennacooks, and had taken her to his home. Their honeymoon was happy, but old ties are strong, and after a little time the bride felt a longing to see her people again. When she made known this wish the husband not only consented to her visit, but gave her a guard of his most trusty hunters who saw her safe in her father's lodge (near the site of Concord, New Hampshire), and returned directly. Presently came a messenger from Passaconaway, informing his son-in-law that Weetamoo had finished her visit and wished again to be with her husband, to whom he looked for an escort to guide her through the wilderness. Winnepurkit felt that his dignity as a chief was slighted by this last request, and he replied that as he had supplied her with a guard for the outward journey it was her father's place to send her back, "for it stood not with Winnepurkit's reputation either to make himself or his men so servile as to fetch her again."

Passaconaway returned a sharp answer that irritated Winnepurkit still more, and he was told by the young sagamore that he might send his daughter or keep her, for she would never be sent for. In this unhappy strife for precedent, which has been repeated on later occasions by princes and society persons, the young wife seemed to be fated as an unwilling sacrifice; but summoning spirit to leave her father's wigwam she launched a canoe on the Merrimack, hoping to make her way along that watery highway to her husband's domain. It was winter, and the stream was full of floating ice; at the best of times it was not easy to keep a frail vessel of bark in the current away from the rapids, and a wandering hunter reported that a canoe had come down the river guided by a woman, that it had swung against the Amoskeag rocks, where Manchester stands now, and a few moments later was in a quieter reach of water, broken and empty. No more was seen of Weetamoo.

Myths and Legends

THE FATAL FORGET-ME-NOT

THREE miles out from the Nahant shore, Massachusetts, rises Egg Rock, a dome of granite topped by a light-house. In the last century the forget-me-nots that grew in a little marsh at its summit were much esteemed, for it was reported that if a girl should receive one of these little flowers from her lover the two would be faithful to each other through all their married life. It was before a temporary separation that a certain young couple strolled together on the Nahant cliffs. The man was to sail for Italy next day, to urge parental consent to their union. As he looked dreamily into the sea the legend of the forget-me-not came into his mind, and in a playful tone he offered to gather a bunch as a memento. Unthinkingly the girl consented. He ran down the cliff to his boat, pushed out, and headed toward the rock, but a fisherman shouted that a gale was rising and the tide was coming in; indeed, the horizon was whitening and the rote was growing plain.

Alice had heard the cry of warning and would have called him back, but she was forsaken by the power of speech, and watched, with pale face and straining eyes, the boat beating smartly across the surges. It was seen to reach Egg Rock, and after a lapse came dancing toward the shore again; but the tide was now swirling in rapidly, the waves were running high, and the wind freshened as the sun

sank. At times the boat was out of sight in the
hollowed water, and as it neared Nahant it became
unmanageable. Apparently it had filled with water
and the tiller-rope had broken. Nothing could be
done by the spectators who had gathered on the
rocks, except to shout directions that were futile,
even if they could be heard. At last the boat was
lifted by a breaker and hurled against a mass of
granite at the very feet of the man's mistress.
When the body was recovered next day, a bunch
of forget-me-not was clasped in the rigid hand.

THE OLD MILL AT SOMERVILLE

THE "old powder-house," as the round stone
tower is called that stands on a gravel ridge
in Somerville, Massachusetts, is so named because at
the outbreak of the Revolutionary War it was used
temporarily as a magazine; but long before that it
was a wind-mill. Here in the old days two lovers
held their tryst: a sturdy and honest young farmer
of the neighborhood and the daughter of a man
whose wealth puffed him with purse-pride. It was
the plebeian state of the farmer that made him look
at him with an unfavorable countenance, and when
it was whispered to him that the young people were
meeting each other almost every evening at the mill,
he resolved to surprise them there and humiliate, if
he did not punish them. From the shadow of the
door they saw his approach, and, yielding to the

girl's imploring, the lover secreted himself while she climbed to the loft. The flutter of her dress caught the old man's eye and he hastened, panting, into the mill. For some moments he groped about, for his eyes had not grown used to the darkness of the place, and hearing his muttered oaths, the girl crept backward from the stair.

She was beginning to hope that she had not been seen, when her foot caught in a loose board and she stumbled, but in her fall she threw out her hand to save herself and found a rope within her grasp. Directly that her weight had been applied to it there was a whir and a clank. The cord had set the great fans in motion. At the same moment a fall was heard, then a cry, passing from anger into anguish. She rushed down the stair, the lover appeared from his hiding-place at the same moment, and together they dragged the old man to his feet. At the moment when the wind had started the sails he had been standing on one of the mill-stones and the sudden jerk had thrown him down. His arm caught between the grinding surfaces and had been crushed to pulp. He was carried home and tenderly nursed, but he did not live long; yet before he died he was made to see the folly of his course, and he consented to the marriage that it had cost him so dear to try to prevent. Before she could summon heart to fix the wedding-day the girl passed many months of grief and repentance, and for the rest of her life she avoided the old mill. There was good reason for doing so, people said, for on windy nights the spirit of the old man used to haunt the place, using such profanity that it became visible in the form of blue lights, dancing and exploding about the building.

EDWARD RANDOLPH'S PORTRAIT

NOTHING is left of Province House, the old home of the royal governors, in Boston, but the gilded Indian that served as its weather-cock and aimed his arrow at the winds from the cupola. The house itself was swept away long ago in the so-called march of improvement. In one of its rooms hung a picture so dark that when Lieu-tenant-Governor Hutchinson went to live there hardly anybody could say what it represented. There were hints that it was a portrait of the devil, painted at a witch-meeting near Salem, and that on the eve of disasters in the province a dread-ful face had glared from the canvas. Shirley had seen it on the night of the fall of Ticonderoga, and servants had gone shuddering from the room, cer-tain that they had caught the glance of a malignant eye.

It was known to the governors, however, that the portrait, if not that of the arch fiend, was that of one who in the popular mind was none the less a devil: Edward Randolph, the traitor, who had re-pealed the first provincial charter and deprived the colonists of their liberties. Under the curse of the people he grew pale and pinched and ugly, his face at last becoming so hateful that men were unwilling to look at it. Then it was that he sat for his portrait. Threescore or odd years afterward, Hutchinson sat in the hall wondering vaguely if coming events would consign him to the obloquy that had fallen on his predecessor, for at his bidding a fleet had come into the harbor with three regiments of red coats on board, despatched from Halifax to overawe the city. The coming of the selectmen to protest against quartering these troops on the people and the substitution of martial for civic law, interrupted his reverie, and a warm debate arose. At last the governor seized his pen impatiently, and cried, " The king is my master and England is my home. Upheld by them, I defy the rabble."

He was about to sign the order for bringing in the troops when a curtain that had hung before the picture was drawn aside. Hutchinson stared at the canvas in amazement, then muttered, " It is Randolph's spirit ! It wears the look of hell." The picture was seen to be that of a man in antique garb, with a despairing, hunted, yet evil expression in the face, and seemed to stare at Hutchinson.

" It is a warning," said one of the company.

Hutchinson recovered himself with an effort and turned away. " It is a trick," he cried ; and bending over the paper he fixed his name, as if in desperate haste. Then he trembled, turned white, and wiped a sweat from his brow. The selectmen departed in silence but in anger, and those who saw Hutchinson on the streets next day affirmed that the portrait had stepped out of its canvas and stood at his side through the night. Afterward, as he lay on his death-bed, he cried that the blood of the Boston massacre was filling his throat, and as his soul passed from him his face, in its agony and rage, was the face of Edward Randolph.

LADY ELEANORE'S MANTLE

LADY ELEANORE ROCHCLIFFE, being orphaned, was admitted to the family of her distant relative, Governor Shute, of Massachusetts Bay, and came to America to take her home with him. She arrived at the gates of Province House, in Boston, in the governor's splendid coach, with outriders and guards, and as the governor went to receive her, a pale young man, with tangled hair, sprang from the crowd and fell in the dust at her feet, offering himself as a footstool for her to tread upon. Her proud face lighted with a smile of scorn, and she put out her hand to stay the governor, who was in the act of striking the fellow with his cane.

"Do not strike him," she said. "When men seek to be trampled, it is a favor they deserve."

For a moment she bore her weight on the prostrate form, "emblem of aristocracy trampling on human sympathies and the kindred of nature," and as she stood there the bell on South Church began to toll for a funeral that was passing at the moment. The crowd started; some looked annoyed; Lady Eleanore remained calm and walked in stately fashion up the passage on the arm of His Excellency. "Who was that insolent fellow?" was asked of Dr. Clarke, the governor's physician.

"Gervase Helwyse," replied the doctor; "a youth of no fortune, but of good mind until he met this lady in London, when he fell in love with her, and her pride and scorn have crazed him."

A few nights after a ball was given in honor of the governor's ward, and Province House was filled with the elect of the city. Commanding in figure, beautiful in face, richly dressed and jewelled, the Lady Eleanore was the admired of the whole assembly, and the women were especially curious to see her mantle, for a rumor went out that it had been made by a dying girl, and had the magic power of giving new beauty to the wearer every time it was put on. While the guests were taking refreshment, a young man stole into the room with a silver goblet, and this he offered on his knee to Lady Eleanore. As she looked down she recognized the face of Helwyse.

"Drink of this sacramental wine," he said, eagerly, "and pass it among the guests."

"Perhaps it is poisoned," whispered a man, and in another moment the liquor was overturned, and Helwyse was roughly dragged away.

Tales of Puritan Land

"Pray, gentlemen, do not hurt my poor admirer," said the lady, in a tone of languor and condescension that was unusual to her. Breaking from his captives, Helwyse ran back and begged her to cast her mantle into the fire. She replied by throwing a fold of it above her head and smiling as she said, "Farewell. Remember me as you see me now."

Helwyse shook his head sadly and submitted to be led away. The weariness in Eleanore's manner increased; a flush was burning on her cheek; her laugh had grown infrequent. Dr. Clarke whispered something in the governor's ear that made that gentleman start and look alarmed. It was announced that an unforeseen circumstance made it necessary to close the festival at once, and the company went home. A few days after the city was thrown into a panic by an outbreak of small-pox, a disease that in those times could not be prevented nor often cured, and that gathered its victims by thousands. Graves were dug in rows, and every night the earth was piled hastily on fresh corpses. Before all infected houses hung a red flag of warning, and Province House was the first to show it, for the plague had come to town in Lady Eleanore's mantle. The people cursed her pride and pointed to the flags as her triumphal banners. The pestilence was at its height when Gervase Helwyse appeared in Province House. There were none to stay him now, and he climbed the stairs, peering from room to room, until he entered a darkened chamber, where

Myths and Legends

something stirred feebly under a silken coverlet and
a faint voice begged for water. Helwyse tore apart
the curtains and exclaimed, "Fie! What does such
a thing as you in Lady Eleanore's apartment?"

The figure on the bed tried to hide its hideous
face. "Do not look on me," it cried. "I am
cursed for my pride that I wrapped about me as a
mantle. You are avenged. I am Eleanore Rochcliffe."

The lunatic stared for a moment, then the house
echoed with his laughter. The deadly mantle lay
on a chair. He snatched it up, and waving also the
red flag of the pestilence ran into the street. In a
short time an effigy wrapped in the mantle was
borne to Province House and set on fire by a mob.
From that hour the pest abated and soon disappeared, though graves and scars made a bitter memory of it for many a year. Unhappiest of all was
the disfigured creature who wandered amid the
shadows of Province House, never showing her face,
unloved, avoided, lonely.

HOWE'S MASQUERADE

DURING the siege of Boston Sir William Howe
undertook to show his contempt for the raw
fellows who were disrespectfully tossing cannon-balls
at him from the batteries in Cambridge and South
Boston, by giving a masquerade. It was a brilliant
affair, the belles and blades of the loyalist set being

256

present, some in the garb of their ancestors, for the past is ever more picturesque than the present, and a few roisterers caricaturing the American generals in ragged clothes, false noses, and absurd wigs. At the height of the merriment a sound of a dirge echoing through the streets caused the dance to stop. The funeral music paused before the doors of Province House, where the dance was going on, and they were flung open. Muffled drums marked time for a company that began to file down the great stair from the floor above the ball-room: dark men in steeple-hats and pointed beards, with Bibles, swords, and scrolls, who looked sternly at the guests and descended to the street.

Colonel Joliffe, a Whig, whose age and infirmity had prevented him from joining Washington, and whose courtesy and intelligence had made him respected by his foes, acted as chorus: " These I take to be the Puritan governors of Massachusetts: Endicott, Winthrop, Vane, Dudley, Haynes, Bellingham, Leverett, Bradstreet." Then came a rude soldier, mailed, begirt with arms: the tyrant Andros; a brown-faced man with a sailor's gait: Sir William Phipps; a courtier wigged and jewelled: Earl Bellomont; the crafty, well-mannered Dudley; the twinkling, red-nosed Shute; the ponderous Burnet; the gouty Belcher; Shirley, Pownall, Bernard, Hutchinson; then a soldier, whose cocked hat he held before his face. " 'Tis the shape of Gage !" cried an officer, turning pale. The lights were dull and an uncomfortable silence had fallen on the company. Last, came a tall man muffled in a military cloak, and as he paused on the landing the guests looked from him to their host in amazement, for it was the figure of Howe himself. The governor's patience was at an end, for this was a part of the masquerade that had not been looked for. He fiercely cried to Joliffe, " There is a plot in this. Your head has stood too long on a traitor's shoulders."

" Make haste to cut it off, then," was the reply, " for the power of Sir William Howe and of the king, his master, is at an end. These shadows are mourners at his funeral. Look! The last of the governors."

Howe rushed with drawn sword on the figure of himself, when it turned and looked at him. The blade clanged to the floor and Howe fell back with a gasp of horror, for the face was his own. Hand nor voice was raised to stay the double-goer as it mournfully passed on. At the threshold it stamped its foot and shook its fists in air; then the door closed. Mingled with the strains of the funeral march, as it died along the empty streets, came the tolling of the bell on South Church steeple, striking the hour of midnight. The festivities were at an end and, oppressed by a nameless fear, the spectators of this strange pageant made ready for departure; but before they left the booming of cannon at the south-ward announced that Washington had advanced. The glories of Province House were over. When the last of the royal governors left it he paused on the threshold, beat his foot on the stone, and flung up his hands in an attitude of grief and rage.

OLD ESTHER DUDLEY

BOSTON had surrendered. Washington was advancing from the heights where he had trained his guns on the British works, and Sir William Howe lingered at the door of Province House, —last of the royal governors who would stand there, —and cursed and waved his hands and beat his heel on the step, as if he were crushing rebellion by that act. The sound brought an old woman to his side. "Esther Dudley!" he exclaimed. "Why are you not gone?"

"I shall never leave. As housekeeper for the governors and pensioner of the king, this has been my home; the only home I know. Go back, but send more troops. I will keep the house till you return."

"Grant that I may return," he cried. "Since you will stay, take this bag of guineas and keep this key until a governor shall demand it."

Then, with fierce and moody brow, the governor went forth, and the faded eyes of Esther Dudley saw him nevermore. When the soldiers of the republic cast about for quarters in Boston town, they spared the official mansion to this old woman. Her bridling toryism and assumption of old state amused them and did no harm; indeed, her loyalty was half admired; beside, nobody took the pride in the place that she did, or would keep it in better order. That she sometimes had a half-dozen of unrepentant codgers in to dinner, and that they were suspected of drinking healths to George III. in crusted port, was a fact to blink. Rumor had it that not all her guests were flesh and blood, but that she had an antique mirror across which ancient occupants of the house would pass in shadowy procession at her command, and that she was wont to have the Shirleys, Olivers, Hutchinsons, and Dudleys out of their graves to hold receptions there; so a touch of dread may have mingled in the feeling that kept the populace aloof.

Living thus by herself, refusing to hear of rebel victories, construing the bonfires, drumming, hurrahs, and bell-ringing to signify fresh triumphs for England, she drifted farther and farther out of her time and existed in the shadows of the past. She lighted the windows for the king's birthday, and often from the cupola watched for a British fleet, heeding not the people below, who, as they saw her withered face, repeated the prophecy, with a laugh: " When the golden Indian on Province House shall shoot his arrow and the cock on South Church spire shall crow, look for a royal governor again." So, when it was bandied about the streets that the governor was coming, she took it in no wise strange, but dressed herself in silk and hoops, with store of ancient jewels, and made ready to receive him. In truth, there was a function, for already a man of stately mien, and richly dressed, was advancing through the court, with a staff of men in wigs and laced coats behind him, and a company of troops at a little distance. Esther Dudley flung the door wide and dropping on her knees held forth the key with the cry, " Thank heaven for this hour! God save the king !"

The governor put off his hat and helped the woman to her feet. " A strange prayer," said he ; " yet we will echo it to this effect: For the good of the realm that still owns him to be its ruler, God save King George."

Esther Dudley stared wildly. That face she remembered now,—the proscribed rebel, John Hancock; governor, not by royal grant, but by the people's will.

" Have I welcomed a traitor ? Then let me die."

" Alas ! Mistress Dudley, the world has changed for you in these later years. America has no king." He offered her his arm, and she clung to it for a moment, then, sinking down, the great key, that she so long had treasured, clanked to the floor.

" I have been faithful unto death," she gasped. " God save the king !"

The people uncovered, for she was dead.

" At her tomb," said Hancock, " we will bid farewell forever to the past. A new day has come for us. In its broad light we will press onward."

Myths and Legends

THE LOSS OF JACOB HURD

JACOB HURD, stern witch-harrier of Ipswich, can abide nothing out of the ordinary course of things, whether it be flight on a broomstick or the wrong adding of figures; so his son gives him trouble, for he is an imaginative boy, who walks alone, talking to the birds, making rhymes, picking flowers, and dreaming. That he will never be a farmer, mechanic, or tradesman is as good as certain, and one day when the child runs in with a story of a golden horse, with tail and mane of silver, on which he has ridden over land and sea, climbing mountains and swimming rivers, he turns pale with fright lest the boy be bewitched; then, as the awfulness of the invention becomes manifest, he cries, " Thou knowest thou art lying," and strikes the little fellow.

The boy staggers into his mother's arms, and that night falls into a fever, in which he raves of his horse and the places he will see, while Jacob sits by his side, too sore in heart for words, and he never leaves the cot for food or sleep till the fever is burned out. Just before he closes his eyes the child looks about him and says that he hears the horse pawing in the road, and, either for dust or cloud or sun gleam, it seems for an instant as if the horse were there. The boy gives a cry of joy, then sinks upon his pillow, lifeless.

Some time after this Jacob sets off one morning,

while the stars are out, to see three witches hanged, but at evening his horse comes flying up the road, splashed with blood and foam, and the neighbors know from that of Jacob's death, for he is lying by the wayside with an Indian arrow in his heart and an axe-mark on his head. The wife runs to the door, and, though she shakes with fear at its approach, she sees that in the sunset glow the horse's sides have a shine like gold, and its mane and tail are silver white. Now the animal is before the house, but the woman does not faint or cry at the blood splash on the saddle, for—is it the dust-cloud that takes that shape?— she sees on its back a boy with a shining face, who throws a kiss at her,—her Paul. He, little poet, lives in spirit, and has found happiness.

THE HOBOMAK

SUCH was the Indian name of the site of Westboro, Massachusetts, and the neighboring pond was Hochomocko. The camp of the red men near the shore was full of bustle one day, for their belle, Iano, was to marry the young chief, Sassacus. The feast was spread and all were ready to partake of it, when it was found that the bride was missing. One girl had seen her steal into the wood with a roguish smile on her lip, and knew that she intended to play hide-and-seek with Sassacus before she should be proclaimed a wife, but the day wore on and she did not come. Among those who were late in reaching camp was Wequoash, who brought a panther in that he had slain on Boston Hill, and he bragged about his skill, as usual. There had been a time when he was a rival of the chief for the hand of Iano, and he showed surprise and concern at her continued absence. The search went on for two days, and, at the end of that time, the girl's body was taken from the lake.

At the funeral none groaned so piteously as Wequoash. Yet Sassacus felt his loss so keenly that he fell into a sickness next day, and none was found so constant in his ministrations as Wequoash; but all to no avail, for within a week Sassacus, too, was dead. As the strongest and bravest remaining in the tribe, Wequoash became heir to his honors by election.

A year later he sat moodily by the lakeside, when a flame burst up from the water, and a canoe floated toward him that a mysterious agency impelled him to enter. The boat sped toward the flame, that, at his approach, assumed Iano's form. He heard the water gurgle as he passed over the spot where the shape had glimmered, but there was no other sound or check. Next year this thing occurred again, and then the spirit spoke: "Only once more."

Yet a third time his fate took him to the spot, and as the hour came on he called his people to him: "This," said he, "is my death-day. I have done evil, and the time comes none too soon. Sassacus was your chief. I envied him his happiness, and gave him poison when I nursed him. Worse than that, I saw Iano in her canoe on her wedding-day. She had refused my hand. I entered my canoe and chased her over the water, in pretended sport, but in the middle of the lake I upset her birch and she was drowned. See! she comes!"

For, as he spoke, the light danced up again, and the boat came, self-impelled, to the strand. We-quoash entered it, and with head bent down was hurried away. Those on the shore saw the flame condense to a woman's shape, and a voice issued from it : "It is my hour!" A blinding bolt of lightning fell, and at the appalling roar of thunder all hid their faces. When they looked up, boat and flame had vanished. Whenever, afterward, an Indian rowed across the place where the murderer had sunk, he dropped a stone, and the monument that grew in that way can be seen on the pond floor to this day.

BERKSHIRE TORIES

THE tories of Berkshire, Massachusetts, were men who had been endeared to the king by holding office under warrant from that sacred personage. They have been gently dealt with by historians, but that is "overstrained magnanimity which concentrates its charities and praises for defeated champions of the wrong, and reserves its censures for triumphant defenders of the right." While the following incidents have been so well avouched that they deserve to stand as history, their picturesqueness justifies renewed acquaintance.

Among the loyalists was Gideon Smith, of Stock-bridge, who had helped British prisoners to escape, and had otherwise made himself so obnoxious that he was forced for a time to withdraw and pass a season of penitence and meditation in a cavern near Lenox, that is called the Tories' Glen. Here he lay for weeks, none but his wife knowing where he was, but at his request she walked out every day with her children, leading them past his cave, where he fed on their faces with hungry eyes. They prattled on, never dreaming that their father was but a few feet from them. Smith survived the war and lived to be on good terms with his old foes.

In Lenox lived a Tory, one of those respectable buffers to whom wealth and family had given immunity in the early years of the war, but who sorely tried the temper of his neighbors by damning everything American from Washington downward. At last they could endure his abuse no longer; his example had affected other Anglomaniacs, and a committee waited on him to tell him that he could either swear allegiance to the colonies or be hanged. He said he would be hanged if he would swear, or words to that effect, and hanged he was, on a ready-made gallows in the street. He was let down shortly, "brought around" with rum, and the oath was offered again. He refused it. This had not been

Tales of Puritan Land

looked for. It had been taken for granted that he
would abjure his fealty to the king at the first tight-
ening of the cord. A conference was held, and it
was declared that retreat would be undignified and
unsafe, so the Tory was swung up again, this time
with a yank that seemed to " mean business." He
hung for some time, and when lowered gave no sign
of life. There was some show of alarm at this, for
nobody wanted to kill the old fellow, and every
effort was made to restore consciousness. At last
the lungs heaved, the purple faded from his cheek,
his eyes opened, and he gasped, " I'll swear." With
a shout of joy the company hurried him to the
tavern, seated him before the fire, and put a glass of
punch in his hand. He drank the punch to Washington's health, and after a time was heard to re-
mark to himself, " It's a hard way to make Whigs,
but it'll do it."

Nathan Jackson, of Tyringham, was another
Yankee who had seen fit to take arms against his
countrymen, and when captured he was charged
with treason and remanded for trial. The jail, in
Great Barrington, was so little used in those days of
sturdy virtue that it had become a mere shed, fit to
hold nobody, and Jackson, after being locked into it,
might have walked out whenever he felt disposed ;
but escape, he thought, would have been a confession of the wrongness of Tory principles, or of a
fear to stand trial. He found life so monotonous,
however, that he asked the sheriff to let him go out

to work during the day, promising to sleep in his cell, and such was his reputation for honesty that his request was granted without a demur, the prisoner returning every night to be locked up. When the time approached for the court to meet in Springfield heavy harvesting had begun, and, as there was no other case from Berkshire County to present, the sheriff grumbled at the bother of taking his prisoner across fifty miles of rough country, but Jackson said that he would make it all right by going alone. The sheriff was glad to be released from this duty, so off went the Tory to give himself up and be tried for his life. On the way he was overtaken by Mr. Edwards, of the Executive Council, then about to meet in Boston, and without telling his own name or office, he learned the extraordinary errand of this lonely pedestrian. Jackson was tried, admitted the charges against him, and was sentenced to death. While he awaited execution of the law upon him, the council in Boston received petitions for clemency, and Mr. Edwards asked if there was none in favor of Nathan Jackson. There was none. Mr. Edwards related the circumstance of his meeting with the condemned man, and a murmur of surprise and admiration went around the room. A despatch was sent to Springfield. When it reached there the prison door was flung open and Jackson walked forth free.

Tales of Puritan Land

THE REVENGE OF JOSIAH BREEZE

TWO thousand Cape Cod fishermen had gone to join the colonial army, and·in their absence the British ships had run in shore to land crews on mischievous errands. No man, woman, or child on the Cape but hated the troops and sailors of King George, and would do anything to work them harm. When the Somerset was wrecked off Truro, in 1778, the crew were helped ashore, 'tis true, but they were straightway marched to prison, and it was thought that no other frigate would venture near the shifting dunes where she had laid her skeleton, as many a good ship had done before and has done since. It was November, and ugly weather was shutting in, when a three-decker, that had been tacking off shore and that flew the red flag, was seen to yaw wildly while reefing sail and drift toward land with a broken tiller. No warning signal was raised on the bluffs; not a hand was stirred to rescue. Those who saw the accident watched with sullen satisfaction the on-coming of the vessel, nor did they cease to look for disaster when the ship anchored and stowed sail.

Ezekiel and Josiah Breeze, father and son, stood at the door of their cottage and watched her peril until three lights twinkling faintly through the gray of driving snow were all that showed where the enemy lay, straining at her cables and tossing on a wrathful sea. They stood long in silence, but at last the boy exclaimed, " I'm going to the ship."

" If you stir from here, you're no son of mine," said Ezekiel.

" But she's in danger, dad."

" As she oughter be. By mornin' she'll be strewed along the shore and not a spar to mark where she's a-swingin' now."

" And the men ?"

" It's a jedgment, boy."

The lad remembered how the sailors of the Ajax had come ashore to burn the homes of peaceful fishermen and farmers ; how women had been insulted ; how his friends and mates had been cut down at Long Island with British lead and steel ; how, when he ran to warn away a red-faced fellow that was robbing his garden, the man had struck him on the shoulder with a cutlass. He had sworn then to be revenged. But to let a host go down to death and never lift a helping hand—was that a fair revenge ? " I've got to go, dad," he burst forth. " To-morrow morning there'll be five hundred faces turned up on the beach, covered with ice and staring at the sky, and five hundred mothers in England will wonder when they're goin' to see those faces again. If ever they looked at me the sight of 'em would never go out of my eyes. I'd be harnted by 'em, awake and asleep. And to-morrow is Thanksgiving. I've got to go, dad, and I will." So speaking, he rushed away and was swallowed in the gloom.

Tales of Puritan Land

The man stared after him; then, with a revulsion of feeling, he cried, " You're right, 'Siah. I'll go with you." But had he called in tones of thunder he would not have been heard in the roar of the wind and crash of the surf. As he reached the shore he saw faintly on the phosphorescent foam a something that climbed a hill of water; it was lost over its crest and reappeared on the wave beyond; it showed for a moment on the third wave, then it vanished in the night. "Josiah!" It was a long, querulous cry. No answer. In half an hour a thing rode by the watcher on the sands and fell with a crash beside him—a boat bottom up: his son's.

Next day broke clear, with new snow on the ground. In his house at Provincetown, Captain Breeze was astir betimes, for his son Ezekiel, his grandson Josiah, and all other relatives who were not at the front with Washington were coming for the family reunion. Plump turkeys were ready for the roasting, great loaves of bread and cake stood beside the oven, redoubtable pies of pumpkin and apple filled the air with maddening odors. The people gathered and chattered around his cheery fire of the damage that the storm had done, when Ezekiel stumbled in, his brown face haggard, his lips working, and a tremor in his hands. He said, "Josiah!" in a thick voice, then leaned his arms against the chimney and pressed his face upon them. Among fishermen whose lives are in daily peril the understanding of misfortune is quick, and the old man put

271

his hand on the shoulder of his son and bent his head. The day of joy was become a day of gloom. As the news went out, the house began to fill with sympathizing friends, and there was talking in low voices through the rooms, when a cry of surprise was heard outside. A ship, cased in tons of ice, was forging up the harbor, her decks swarming with blue jackets, some of whom were beating off the frozen masses from lower spars and rigging. She followed the channel so steadily, it was plain to be seen that a wise hand was at her helm ; her anchor ran out and she swung on the tide. "The Ajax, as I'm a sinner!" exclaimed a sailor on shore. A boat put off from her, and people angrily collected at the wharf, with talk of getting out their guns, when a boyish figure arose in the stern, and was greeted with a shout of surprise and welcome.

The boat touched the beach, Josiah Breeze leaped out of it, and in another minute his father had him in a bear's embrace, making no attempt to stop the tears that welled out of his eyes. An officer had followed Josiah on shore, and going to the group he said, "That boy is one to be proud of. He put out in a sea that few men could face, to save an enemy's ship and pilot it into the harbor. I could do no less than bring him back." There was praise and laughter and clasping of hands, and when the Thanksgiving dinner was placed, smoking, on the board, the commander of H. M. S. Ajax was among the jolliest of the guests at Captain Breeze's table.

Tales of Puritan Land

THE MAY-POLE OF MERRYMOUNT

THE people of Merrymount—unsanctified in the eyes of their Puritan neighbors, for were they not Episcopals, who had pancakes at Shrovetide and wassail at Christmas?—were dancing about their May-pole one summer evening, for they tried to make it May throughout the year. Some were masked like animals, and all were tricked with flowers and ribbons. Within their circle, sharing in song and jest, were the lord and lady of the revels, and an English clergyman waiting to join the pair in wedlock. Life, they sang, should be all jollity: away with care and duty; leave wisdom to the weak and old, and sanctity for fools. Watching the sport from a neighboring wood stood a band of frowning Puritans, and as the sun set they stalked forth and broke through the circle. All was dismay. The bells, the laughter, the song were silent, and some who had tasted Puritan wrath before shrewdly smelled the stocks. A Puritan of iron face—it was Endicott, who had cut the cross from the flag of England—warning aside the "priest of Baal," proceeded to hack the pole down with his sword. A few swinging blows, and down it sank, with its ribbons and flowers.

"So shall fall the pride of vain people; so shall come to grief the preachers of false religion," quoth he. "Truss those fellows to the trees and give them half a dozen of blows apiece as token that we brook no ungodly conduct and hostility to our liberties. And you, king and queen of the May, have you no better things to think about than fiddling and dancing? How if I punish you both?"

"Had I the power I'd punish you for saying it," answered the swain; "but, as I have not, I am compelled to ask that the girl go unharmed."

"Will you have it so, or will you share your lover's punishment?" asked Endicott.

"I will take all upon myself," said the woman.

The face of the governor softened. "Let the young fellow's hair be cut, in pumpkin-shell fashion," he commanded; "then bring them to me—but gently."

He was obeyed, and as the couple came before him, hand in hand, he took a chain of roses from the fallen pole and cast it about their necks. And so they were married. Love had softened rigor and all were better for the assertion of a common humanity. But the May-pole of Merrymount was never set up again. There were no more games and plays and dances, nor singing of worldly music. The town went to ruin, the merrymakers were scattered, and the gray sobriety of religion and toil fell on Pilgrim land again.

Tales of Puritan Land

THE DEVIL AND TOM WALKER

WHEN Charles River was lined with groves and marshes there lived in a cabin, near Brighton, Massachusetts, an ill-fed rascal named Tom Walker. There was but one in the commonwealth who was more penurious, and that was his wife. They squabbled over the spending of a penny and each grudged food to the other. One day as Tom walked through the pine wood near his place, by habit watching the ground—for even there a farthing might be discovered—he prodded his stick into a skull, cloven deep by an Indian tomahawk. He kicked it, to shake the dirt off, when a gruff voice spake : " What are you doing in my grounds ?" A swarthy fellow, with the face of a charcoal burner, sat on a stump, and Tom wondered that he had not seen him as he approached.

He replied, " Your grounds ! They belong to Deacon Peabody."

" Deacon Peabody be damned !" cried the black fellow ; " as I think he will be, anyhow, if he does not look after his own sins a little sharper and a little less curiously after his neighbors'. Look, if you want to see how he is faring," and, pointing to a tree, he called Tom to notice that the deacon's name was written on the bark and that it was rotten at the core. To his surprise, Tom found that nearly every tree had the name of some prominent man cut upon it.

"Who are you?" he asked.

"I go by different names in different places," replied the dark one. "In some countries I am the black miner; in some the wild huntsman; here I am the black woodman. I am the patron of slave dealers and master of Salem witches."

"I think you are the devil," blurted Tom.

"At your service," replied his majesty.

Now, Tom, having lived long with Mrs. Walker, had no fear of the devil, and he stopped to have a talk with him. The devil remarked, in a careless tone, that Captain Kidd had buried his treasure in that wood, under his majesty's charge, and that whoever wished could find and keep it by making the usual concession. This Tom declined. He told his wife about it, however, and she was angry with him for not having closed the bargain at once, declaring that if he had not courage enough to add this treasure to their possessions she would not hesitate to do it. Tom showed no disposition to check her. If she got the money he would try to get a share of it, and if the devil took away his helpmate—well, there were things that he had made his mind to endure, when he had to. True enough, the woman started for the wood before sundown, with her spoons in her apron. When Tom discovered that the spoons were gone he, too, set off, for he wanted those back, anyway; but he did not overtake his wife. An apron was found in a tree containing a dried liver and a withered heart, and near that place the earth had been trampled and strewn with handfuls of coarse hair that reminded Tom of the man that he had met in the woods. "Egad!" he muttered, "Old Nick must have had a tough time with her." Half in gratitude and half in curiosity, Tom waited to speak to the dark man, and was next day rewarded by seeing that personage come through the wood with an axe, whistling carelessly. Tom at once approached him on the subject of the buried treasure—not the vanished wife, for her he no longer regarded as a treasure.

After some haggling the devil proposed that Tom should start a loan office in Boston and use Kidd's money in exacting usury. This suited Tom, who promised to screw four per cent. a month out of the unfortunates who might ask his aid, and he was seen to start for town with a bag which his neighbors thought to hold his crop of starveling turnips, but which was really a king's ransom in gold and jewels —the earnings of Captain Kidd in long years of honest piracy. It was in Governor Belcher's time, and cash was scarce. Merchants and professional men as well as the thriftless went to Tom for money, and, as he always had it, his business grew until he seemed to have a mortgage on half the men in Boston who were rich enough to be in debt. He even went so far as to move into a new house, to ride in his own carriage, and to eat enough to keep body and soul together, for he did not want to give up his soul to the one who would claim it—just yet.

Myths and Legends

The most singular proof of his thrift—showing that he wanted to save soul and money both—was shown in his joining the church and becoming a prayerful Christian. He kept a Bible in his pocket and another on his desk, resolved to be prepared if a certain gentleman should call. He buried his old horse feet uppermost, for he was taught that on resurrection day the world would be turned upside down, and he was resolved, if his enemy appeared, to give him a run for it. While employed one afternoon in the congenial task of foreclosing a mortgage his creditor begged for another day to raise the money. Tom was irritable on account of the hot weather and talked to him as a good man of the church ought not to do.

"You have made so much money out of me," wailed the victim of Tom's philanthropies.

"Now, the devil take me if I have made a farthing!" exclaimed Tom.

At that instant there were three knocks at the door, and, stepping out to see who was there, the money lender found himself in presence of his fate. His little Bible was in a coat on a nail, and the bigger one was on his desk. He was without defence. The evil one caught him up like a child, had him on the back of his snorting steed in no time, and giving the beast a cut he flew like the wind in the teeth of a rising storm toward the marshes of Brighton. As he reached there a lightning flash descended into the wood and set it on fire. At the

same moment Tom's house was discovered to be in
flames. When his effects were examined nothing
was found in his strong boxes but cinders and
shavings.

THE GRAY CHAMPION

IT befell Sir Edmund Andros to make himself the
most hated of the governors sent to represent
the king in New England. A spirit of independence, born of a free soil, was already moving in
the people's hearts, and the harsh edicts of this
officer, as well as the oppressive measures of his
master, brought him into continual conflict with the
people. He it was who went to Hartford to demand the surrender of the liberties of that colony.
The lights were blown out and the patent of those
liberties was hurried away from under his nose and
hidden from his reach in a hollow of the Charter
Oak.

In Boston, too, he could call no American his
friend, and it was there that he met one of the first
checks to his arrogance. It was an April evening in
1689, and there was an unusual stir in the streets.
People were talking in low tones, and one caught
such phrases as, "If the Prince of Orange is successful, this Andros will lose his head." "Our
pastors are to be burned alive in King Street."
"The pope has ordered Andros to celebrate the
eve of St. Bartholomew in Boston: we are to be
killed." "Our old Governor Bradstreet is in town,

and Andros fears him." While talk was running in this excited strain the sound of a drum was heard coming through Cornhill. Now was seen a file of soldiers with guns on shoulder, matches twinkling in the falling twilight, and behind them, on horseback, Andros and his councillors, including the priest of King's Chapel, all wearing crucifixes at their throats, all flushed with wine, all looking down with indifference at the people in their dark cloaks and broad-brimmed hats, who looked back at them with suspicion and hate. The soldiers trod the streets like men unused to giving way, and the crowd fell back, pressed against the buildings. Groans and hisses were heard, and a voice sent up this cry, " Lord of Hosts, provide a champion for thy people !"

Ere the echo of that call had ceased there came from the other end of the street, stepping as in time to the drum, an aged man, in cloak and steeple hat, with heavy sword at his thigh. His port was that of a king, and his dignity was heightened by a snowy beard that fell to his waist. Taking the middle of the way he marched on until he was but a few paces from the advancing column. None knew him and he seemed to recognize none among the crowd. As he drew himself to his height, it seemed in the dusk as if he were of no mortal mould. His eye blazed, he thrust his staff before him, and in a voice of invincible command cried, " Halt !"

Half because it was habit to obey the word, half because they were cowed by the majestic presence, the guard stood still and the drum was silenced. Andros spurred forward, but even he made a pause when he saw the staff levelled at his breast. "Forward!" he blustered. "Trample the dotard into the street. How dare you stop the king's governor?"

"I have stayed the march of a king himself," was the answer. "The king you serve no longer sits on the throne of England. To-morrow you will be a prisoner. Back, lest you reach the scaffold!"

A moment of hesitation on Andros's part encouraged the people to press closer, and many of them took no pains to hide the swords and pistols that were girt upon them. The groans and hisses sounded louder. "Down with Andros! Death to tyrants! A curse on King James!" came from among the throng, and some of them stooped as if to tear up the pavings. Doubtful, yet overawed, the governor wheeled about and gloomily marched back through the streets where he had ridden so arrogantly. In truth, his next night was spent in prison, for James had fled from England, and William held the throne. All eyes being on the retreating company, the champion of the people was not seen to depart, but when they turned to praise and thank him he had vanished, and there were those who said that he had melted into twilight.

The incident had passed into legend, and fourscore years had followed it, when the soldiers of another king of England marched down State Street, and fired on the people of Boston who were gathered below the old State House. Again it was said that the form of a tall, white-bearded man in antique garb was seen in that street, warning back the troops and encouraging the people to resist them. On the little field of Lexington in early dawn, and at the breastwork on Bunker Hill, where farmers worked by lantern-light, this dark form was seen—the spirit of New England. And it is told that whenever any foreign foe or domestic oppressor shall dare the temper of the people, in the van of the resisting army shall be found this champion.

THE FOREST SMITHY

EARLY in this century a man named Ainsley appeared at Holyoke, Massachusetts, and set up a forge in a wood at the edge of the village, with a two-room cottage to live in. A Yankee peddler once put up at his place for shelter from a storm, and as the rain increased with every hour he begged to remain in the house over night, promising to pay for his accommodation in the morning. The blacksmith, who seemed a mild, considerate man, said that he was willing, but that, as the rooms were small, it would be well to refer the matter to his wife. As the peddler entered the house the wife—a weary-looking woman with white hair—seated herself at once in a thickly-cushioned arm-chair, and, as if loath to leave it, told the peddler that if he would put up with simple fare and a narrow berth he was welcome. After a candle had been lighted the three sat together for some time, talking of crops and trade, when there came a rush of hoofs without and a hard-looking man, who had dismounted at the door, entered without knocking. The blacksmith turned pale and the wife's face expressed sore anxiety.

"What brings you here?" asked the smith.

"I must pass the night here," answered the man.

"But, stranger, I can't accommodate you. We have but one spare room, and that has been taken by the man who is sitting there."

"Then give me a bit to eat."

"Get the stranger something," said the woman to her husband, without rising.

"Are you lame, that you don't get it yourself?"

The woman paused; then said, "Husband, you are tired. Sit here and I will wait on the stranger."

The blacksmith took the seat, when the stranger again blustered, "It would be courtesy to offer me that chair, tired as I am. Perhaps you don't know that I am an officer of the law?"

When supper was ready they took their places, the woman drawing up the arm-chair for her own use, but, as the custom was, they all knelt to say grace, and while their faces were buried in their hands the candle was blown out. The stranger jumped up and began walking around the room. When a light could be found he had gone and the cushion had disappeared from the chair. "Oh!

After all these years!" wailed the woman, and falling on her knees she sobbed like a child, while her
husband in vain tried to comfort her. The peddler,
who had already gone to bed, but who had seen a
part of this puzzling drama through the open door,
knew not what to do, but, feeling some concern for
the safety of his own possessions, he drew his pack
into bed with him, and, being tired, fell asleep with
the sobs of the woman sounding in his ears.

When he awoke it was broad day and the earth
was fresh and bright from its bath. After dressing
he passed into the other room, finding the table still
set, the chair before it without its cushion, the fire
out, and nobody in or about the house. The smithy
was deserted, and to his call there was no response
but the chattering of jays in the trees; so, shoulder-
ing his pack, he resumed his journey. He opened
his pack at a farm-house to repair a clock, when he
discovered that his watches were gone, and immediately lodged complaint with the sheriff, but nothing was ever seen again of Ainsley, his wife, or the
rough stranger. Who was the thief? What was
in the cushion? And what brought the stranger to
the house?

WAHCONAH FALLS

THE pleasant valley of Dalton, in the Berkshire
Hills, had been under the rule of Miacomo
for forty years when a Mohawk dignitary of fifty
scalps and fifty winters came a-wooing his daughter

Wahconah. On a June day in 1637, as the girl sat beside the cascade that bears her name, twining flowers in her hair and watching leaves float down the stream, she became conscious of a pair of eyes bent on her from a neighboring coppice, and arose in some alarm. Finding himself discovered, the owner of the eyes, a handsome young fellow, stepped forward with a quieting air of friendliness, and exclaimed, " Hail, Bright Star !"

" Hail, brother," answered Wahconah.

" I am Nessacus," said the man, " one of King Philip's soldiers. Nessacus is tired with his flight from the Long Knives (the English), and his people faint. Will Bright Star's people shut their lodges against him and his friends ?"

The maiden answered, " My father is absent, in council with the Mohawks, but his wigwams are always open. Follow."

Nessacus gave a signal, and forth from the wood came a sad-eyed, battle-worn troop that mustered about him. Under the girl's lead they went down to the valley and were hospitably housed. Five days later Miacomo returned, with him the elderly Mohawk lover, and a priest, Tashmu, of repute a cringing schemer, with whom hunters and soldiers could have nothing in common, and whom they would gladly have put out of the way had they not been deterred by superstitious fears. The strangers were welcomed, though Tashmu looked at them gloomily, and there were games in their honor,

Myths and Legends

Nessacus usually proving the winner, to Wahconah's joy, for she and the young warrior had fallen in love at first sight, and it was not long before he asked her father for her hand. Miacomo favored the suit, but the priest advised him, for politic reasons, to give the girl to the old Mohawk, and thereby cement a tribal friendship that in those days of English aggression might be needful. The Mohawk had three wives already, but he was determined to add Wahconah to his collection, and he did his best, with threats and flattery, to enforce his suit. Nessacus offered to decide the matter in a duel with his rival, and the challenge was accepted, but the wily Tashmu discovered in voices of wind and thunder, flight of birds and shape of clouds, such omens that the scared Indians unanimously forbade a resort to arms. " Let the Great Spirit speak," cried Tashmu, and all yielded their consent.

Invoking a ban on any who should follow, Tashmu proclaimed that he would pass that night in Wizard's Glen, where, by invocations, he would learn the divine will. At sunset he stalked forth, but he had not gone far ere the Mohawk joined him, and the twain proceeded to Wahconah Falls. There was no time for magical hocus-pocus that night, for both of them toiled sorely in deepening a portion of the stream bed, so that the current ran more swiftly and freely on that side, and in the morning Tashmu announced in what way the Great Spirit would show his choice. Assembling the tribe on the river-bank, below a rock that midway split the current, a canoe, with symbols painted on it, was set afloat near the falls. If it passed the dividing rock on the side where Nessacus waited, he should have Wahconah. If it swerved to the opposite shore, where the Mohawk and his counsellor stood, the Great Spirit had chosen the old chief for her husband. Of course, the Mohawk stood on the deeper side. On came the little boat, keeping the centre of the stream. It struck the rock, and all looked eagerly, though Tashmu and the Mohawk could hardly suppress an exultant smile. A little wave struck the canoe: it pivoted against the rock and drifted to the feet of Nessacus. A look of blank amazement came over the faces of the defeated wooer and his friend, while a shout of gladness went up, that the Great Spirit had decided so well. The young couple were wed with rejoicings; the Mohawk trudged homeward, and, to the general satisfaction, Tashmu disappeared with him. Later, when Tashmu was identified as the one who had guided Major Talcott's soldiers to the valley, the priest was caught and slain by Miacomo's men.

KNOCKING AT THE TOMB

KNOCK, knock, knock! The bell has just gone twelve, and there is the clang again upon the iron door of the tomb. The few people of Lanesboro who are paying the penance of misdeeds or late suppers, by lying awake at that dread hour, gather their blankets around their shoulders and mutter a word of prayer for deliverance against unwholesome visitors of the night. Why is the old Berkshire town so troubled? Who is it that lies buried in that tomb, with its ornament of Masonic symbols? Why was the heavy iron knocker placed on the door? The question is asked, but no one will answer it, nor will any say who the woman is that so often visits the cemetery at the stroke of midnight and sounds the call into the chamber of the dead. Starlight, moonlight, or storm—it makes no difference to the woman. There she goes, in her black cloak, seen dim in the night, except where there are snow and moon together, and there she waits, her hand on the knocker, for the bell to strike to set up her clangor. Some say that she is crazy, and it is her freak to do this thing. Is she calling on the corpses to rise and have a dance among the graves? or has she been asked to call the occupant of that house at a given hour? Perhaps, weary of life, she is asking for admittance to the rest and silence of the tomb. She has long been beneath the sod, this troubler of dreams. Who knows her secret?

THE WHITE DEER OF ONOTA

BESIDE quiet Onota, in the Berkshire Hills, dwelt a band of Indians, and while they lived here a white deer often came to drink. So rare was the appearance of an animal like this that its visits were held as good omens, and no hunter of the tribe ever tried to slay it. A prophet of the race had said, "So long as the white doe drinks at Onota, famine shall not blight the Indian's harvest, nor pestilence come nigh his lodge, nor foeman lay waste his country." And this prophecy held true. That summer when the deer came with a fawn as white and graceful as herself, it was a year of great abundance. On the outbreak of the French and Indian War a young officer named Montalbert was despatched to the Berkshire country to persuade the Housatonic Indians to declare hostility to the English, and it was as a guest in the village of Onota that he heard of the white deer. Sundry adventurers had made valuable friendships by returning to the French capital with riches and curiosities from the New World. Even Indians had been abducted as gifts for royalty, and this young ambassador resolved that when he returned to his own country the skin of the white deer should be one of the trophies that would win him a smile from Louis.

He offered a price for it—a price that would have bought all their possessions and miles of the country roundabout, but their deer was sacred, and their refusal to sacrifice it was couched in such indignant terms that he wisely said no more about it in the general hearing. There was in the village a drunken fellow, named Wondo, who had come to that pass when he would almost have sold his soul for liquor, and him the officer led away and plied with rum until he promised to bring the white doe to him. The pretty beast was so familiar with men that she suffered Wondo to catch her and lead her to Montalbert. Making sure that none was near, the officer plunged his sword into her side and the innocent creature fell. The snowy skin, now splashed with red, was quickly stripped off, concealed among the effects in Montalbert's outfit, and he set out for Canada; but he had not been many days on his road before Wondo, in an access of misery and repentance, confessed to his share of the crime that had been done and was slain on the moment.

With the death of the deer came an end to good fortune. Wars, blights, emigration followed, and in a few years not a wigwam was left standing beside Onota.

There is a pendant to this legend, incident to the survival of the deer's white fawn. An English hunter, visiting the lake with dog and gun, was surprised to see on its southern bank a white doe. The animal bent to drink and at the same moment the hunter put his gun to his shoulder. Suddenly a howl was heard, so loud, so long, that the woods echoed it, and the deer, taking alarm, fled like the wind. The howl came from the dog, and, as that animal usually showed sagacity in the presence of game, the hunter was seized with a fear that its form was occupied, for the time, by a hag who lived alone in the "north woods," and who was reputed to have appeared in many shapes—for this was not so long after witch times that their influence was forgotten.

Drawing his ramrod, the man gave his dog such a beating that the poor creature had something worth howling for, because it might be the witch that he was thrashing. Then running to the shanty of the suspected woman he flung open her door and demanded to see her back, for, if she had really changed her shape, every blow that he had given to the dog would have been scored on her skin. When he had made his meaning clear, the crone laid hold on the implement that served her for horse at night, and with the wooden end of it rained blows on him so rapidly that, if the dog had had half the meanness in his nature that some people have, the spectacle would have warmed his heart, for it was a prompt and severe revenge for his sufferings. And to the last the hunter could not decide whether the beating that he received was prompted by indignation or vengeance.

WIZARD'S GLEN

FOUR miles from Pittsfield, Massachusetts, among the Berkshire Hills, is a wild valley, noted for its echoes, that for a century and more has been called Wizard's Glen. Here the Indian priests performed their incantations, and on the red-stained Devil's Altar, it was said, they offered human sacrifice to Hobomocko and his demons of the wood. In Berkshire's early days a hunter, John Chamberlain, of Dalton, who had killed a deer and was carrying it home on his shoulders, was overtaken on the hills by a storm and took shelter from it in a cavernous recess in Wizard's Glen. In spite of his fatigue he was unable to sleep, and while lying on the earth with open eyes he was amazed to see the wood bend apart before him, disclosing a long aisle that was mysteriously lighted and that contained hundreds of capering forms. As his eyes grew accustomed to the faint light he made out tails and cloven feet on the dancing figures ; and one tall form with wings, around whose head a wreath of lightning glittered, and who received the deference of the rest, he surmised to be the devil himself. It was such a night and such a place as Satan and his imps commonly chose for high festivals.

As he lay watching them through the sheeted rain a tall and painted Indian leaped on Devil's Altar, fresh scalps dangling round his body in festoons, and his eyes blazing with fierce command. In a brief incantation he summoned the shadow hordes around him. They came, with torches that burned blue, and went around and around the rock singing a harsh chant, until, at a sign, an Indian girl was dragged in and flung on the block of sacrifice. The figures rushed toward her with extended arms and weapons, and the terrified girl gave one cry that rang in the hunter's ears all his life after. The wizard raised his axe: the devils and vampires gathered to drink the blood and clutch the escaping soul, when in a lightning flash the girl's despairing glance fell on the face of Chamberlain. That look touched his manhood, and drawing forth his Bible he held it toward the rabble while he cried aloud the name of God. There was a crash of thunder. The light faded, the demons vanished, the storm swept past, and peace settled on the hills.

BALANCED ROCK

BALANCED ROCK, or Rolling Rock, near Pittsfield, Massachusetts, is a mass of limestone that was deposited where it stands by the great continental glacier during the ice age, and it weighs four hundred and eighty tons (estimated) in spite of its centuries of weathering. Here one of the Atotarhos, kings of the Six Nations, had his camp. He was a fierce man, who ate and drank from bowls made of the skulls of enemies, and who, when he received messages and petitions, wreathed himself from head to foot with poison snakes. The son of this ferocious being inherited none of his war-like tendencies; indeed, the lad was almost feminine in appearance, and on succeeding to power he applied himself to the cultivation of peaceful arts. Later historians have uttered a suspicion that he was a natural son of Count Frontenac, but that does not suit with this legend.

Myths and Legends

The young Atotarho stood near Balanced Rock watching a number of big boys play duff. In this game one stone is placed upon another and the players, standing as far from it as they fancy they can throw, attempt to knock it out of place with other stones. The silence of Atotarho and his slender, girlish look called forth rude remarks from the boys, who did not know him, and who dared him to test his skill. The young chief came forward, and as he did so the jeers and laughter changed to cries of astonishment and fear, for at each step he grew in size until he towered above them, a giant. Then they knew him, and fell down in dread, but he took no revenge. Catching up great bowlders he tossed them around as easily as if they had been beechnuts, and at last, lifting the balanced rock, he placed it lightly where it stands to-day, gave them a caution against ill manners and hasty judgments, and resumed his slender form. For many years after, the old men of the tribe repeated this story and its lesson from the top of Atotarho's duff.

SHONKEEK-MOONKEEK

THIS is the Mohegan name of the pretty lake in the Berkshires now called Pontoosuc. Shonkeek was a boy, Moonkeek a girl, and they were cousins who grew up as children commonly do, whether in house or wigwam : they roamed the

woods and hills together, filled their baskets with
flowers and berries, and fell in love. But the marriage of cousins was forbidden in the Mohegan
polity, and when they reached an age in which they
found companionship most delightful their rambles
were interdicted and they were even told to avoid
each other. This had the usual effect, and they
met on islands in the lake at frequent intervals, to
the torment of one Nockawando, who wished to
wed the girl himself, and who reported her conduct
to her parents.

The lovers agreed, after this, to fly to an Eastern
tribe into which they would ask to be adopted, but
they were pledged, if aught interfered with their
escape, to meet beneath the lake. Nockawando
interfered. On the next night, as the unsuspecting
Shonkeek was paddling over to the island where the
maid awaited him, the jealous rival, rowing softly
in his wake, sent an arrow into his back, and Shonkeek, without a cry, pitched headlong into the water.
Yet, to the eyes of Nockawando, he appeared to
keep his seat and urge his canoe forward. The girl
saw the boat approach : it sped, now, like an eagle's
flight. One look, as it passed the rock ; one glance
at the murderer, crouching in his birchen vessel,
and with her lover's name on her lips she leaped
into her own canoe and pushed out from shore.
Nockawando heard her raise the death-song and
rowed forward as rapidly as he could, but near the
middle of the lake his arm fell palsied.

Myths and Legends

The song had ended and the night had become strangely, horribly still. Not a chirp of cricket, not a lap of wave, not a rustle of leaf. Motionless the girl awaited, for his boat was still moving by the impetus of his last stroke of the paddle. The evening star was shining low on the horizon, and as her figure loomed in the darkness the star shone through at the point where her eye had looked forth. It was no human creature that sat there. Then came the dead man's boat. The two shadows rowed noiselessly together, and as they disappeared in the mist that was now settling on the landscape, an unearthly laugh rang over the lake; then all was still. When Nockawando reached the camp that night he was a raving maniac. The Indians never found the bodies of the pair, but they believed that while water remains in Pontoosuc its surface will be vexed by these journeys of the dead.

THE SALEM ALCHEMIST

IN 1720 there lived in a turreted house at North and Essex Streets, in Salem, a silent, dark-visaged man,—a reputed chemist. He gathered simples in the fields, and parcels and bottles came and went between him and learned doctors in Boston; but report went around that it was not drugs alone that he worked with, nor medicines for passing ailments that he distilled. The watchman, drowsily pacing the streets in the small hours, saw his shadow move athwart the furnace glare in his tower, and other shadows seemed at the moment to flit about it—shadows that could be thrown by no tangible form, yet that had a grotesque likeness to the human kind. A clink of hammers and a hiss of steam were sometimes heard, and his neighbors devoutly hoped that if he secured the secret of the philosopher's stone or the universal solvent, it would be honestly come by.

But it was neither gold nor the perilous strong water that he wanted. It was life: the elixir that would dispel the chill and decrepitude of age, that would bring back the youthful sparkle to the eye and set the pulses bounding. He explored the surrounding wilderness day after day; the juices of its trees and plants he compounded, night after night, long without avail. Not until after a thousand failures did he conceive that he had secured the ingredients: but they were many, they were perishable, they must be distilled within five days, for fermentation and decay would set in if he delayed longer. Gathering the herbs and piling his floor with fuel, he began his work, alone; the furnace glowed, the retorts bubbled, and through their long throats trickled drops—golden, ruddy, brown, and crystal— that would be combined into that precious draught.

And none too soon, for under the strain of anxiety he seemed to be aging fast. He took no sleep, except while sitting upright in his chair, for, should he yield entirely to nature's appeal, his fire would die and his work be spoiled. With heavy eyes and aching head he watched his furnace and listened to the constant drip, drip of the precious liquor. It was the fourth day. He had knelt to stir his fire to more active burning. Its brightness made him blink, its warmth was grateful, and he reclined before it, with elbow on the floor and head resting on his hand. How cheerily the logs hummed and crackled, yet how drowsily—how slow the hours were—how dull the watch! Lower, lower sank the head, and heavier grew the eyes. At last he lay full length on the floor, and the long sleep of exhaustion had begun.

He was awakened by the sound of a bell. " The church bell!" he cried, starting up. " And people going through the streets to meeting. How is this? The sun is in the east! My God! I have been asleep! The furnace is cold. The elixir!" He hastily blended the essences that he had made, though one or two ingredients were still lacking, and drank them off. " Faugh!" he exclaimed. " Still unfinished—perhaps spoiled. I must begin again." Taking his hat and coat he uttered a weary sigh and was about to open the door when his cheek blenched with pain, sight seemed to leave him, the cry for help that rose to his lips was stifled in a groan of anguish, a groping gesture brought a shelf of retorts and bottles to the floor, and he fell writhing among their fragments. The elixir of life, unfinished, was an elixir of death.

Tales of Puritan Land

ELIZA WHARTON

UNDER the name of Eliza Wharton for a brief time lived a woman whose name was said to be Elizabeth Whitman. Little is known of her, and it is thought that she had gone among strangers to conceal disgrace. She died without telling her story. In 1788 she arrived at the Bell Tavern, Danvers, in company with a man, who, after seeing her properly bestowed, drove away and never returned. A graceful, beautiful, well-bred woman, with face overcast by a tender melancholy, she kept indoors with her books, her sewing, and a guitar, avoiding the gossip of the idle. She said that her husband was absent on a journey, and a letter addressed to " Mrs. Eliza Wharton" was to be seen on her table when she received callers. Once a stranger paused at her door and read the name thereon. As he passed on the woman groaned, " I am undone !" One good woman, seeing her need of care and defiant of village prattling, took her to her home, and there, after giving birth to a dead child, she passed away. Among her effects were letters full of pathetic appeal, and some verses, closing thus :

> " O thou for whose dear sake I bear
> A doom so dreadful, so severe,
> May happy fates thy footsteps guide
> And o'er thy peaceful home preside.
> Nor let Eliza's early tomb
> Infect thee with its baleful gloom."

A stone was raised above her grave, by whom it is not known, and this inscription was engraved thereon: "This humble stone, in memory of Elizabeth Whitman, is inscribed by her weeping friends, to whom she endeared herself by uncommon tenderness and affection. Endowed with superior genius and acquirements, she was still more endeared by humility and benevolence. Let candor throw a veil over her frailties, for great was her charity for others. She sustained the last painful scene far from every friend, and exhibited an example of calm resignation. Her departure was on the 25th of July, 1788, in the thirty-seventh year of her age, and the tears of strangers watered her grave."

SALE OF THE SOUTHWICKS

BITTER were the persecutions endured by Quakers at the hands of the Puritans. They were flogged if they were restless in church, and flogged if they did not go to it. Their ears were slit and they were set in the stocks if they preached, and if any tender-hearted person gave them bed, bite, or sup, he, too, was liable to punishment. They were charged with the awful offence of preaching false doctrine, and no matter how pure their lives might be, the stern Salemite would concede no good of them while their faith was different from his. They even suspected Cobbler Keezar of mischief when he declared that his magic lapstone—

which Agrippa had torn from the tower at Nettes-
heim—gave him a vision of the time when men
would be as glad as nature, when the "snuffler of
psalms" would sing for joy, when priests and Quakers
would talk together kindly, when pillory and gallows
should be gone. Poor Keezar! In ecstasy at that
prospect he flung up his arms, and his lapstone rolled
into the Merrimack. The tired mill-girls of Lowell
still frequent the spot to seek some dim vision of
future comfort.

In contrast to the tales of habitual tyranny toward
the Quakers is the tradition of the Southwicks.
Lawrence and Cassandra, of that name, were ban-
ished from Salem, in spite of their blameless lives,
for they had embraced Quakerism. They died
within three days of each other on Shelter Island,
but their son and daughter, Daniel and Provided,
returned to their birthplace, and were incessantly
fined for not going to church. At last, having lost
their property through seizures made to satisfy their
fines, the General Court of Boston issued an order
for their sale, as slaves, to any Englishman of Virginia or Barbadoes. Edward Butter was assigned to
sell and take them to their master. The day arrived
and Salem market-place was crowded with a throng
of the curious. Provided Southwick mounted the
block and Butter began to call for bids. While ex-
patiating on the aptness of the girl for field- or house-
service, the master of the Barbadoes ship on which
Butter had engaged passage for himself and his two

charges looked into her innocent face, and roared, in noble dudgeon, "If my ship were filled with silver, by God, I'd sink her in harbor rather than take away this child!" The multitude experienced a quick change of feeling and applauded the sentiment. As the judges and officers trudged away with gloomy faces, Provided Southwick descended from the auction-block, and brother and sister went forth into the town free and unharmed.

THE COURTSHIP OF MYLES STANDISH

MYLES STANDISH, compact, hard-headed little captain of the Puritan guard at Plymouth, never knew the meaning of fear until he went a-courting Priscilla Mullins—or was she a Molines, as some say? He had fought white men and red men and never recked of danger in the doing it, but his courage sank to his boots whenever this demure maiden glanced at him, as he thought, with approval. Odd, too, for he had been married once, and Rose was not so long dead that he had forgotten the ways and likings of women; but he made no progress in his suit, and finally chose John Alden to urge it for him. John—who divides with Mary Chilton the honor of being first to land on Plymouth Rock—was a well-favored lad of twenty-two. Until he could build a house for himself he shared Standish's cottage and looked up to that worthy as a guardian, but it was a hard task that was set for him now. He went to goodman Mullins with a slow step and sober countenance and asked leave to plead his protector's cause. The father gave it, called his daughter in, and left them together; then, with noble faith to his mission, the young man begged the maiden's hand for the captain, dwelling on his valor, strength, wisdom, his military greatness, his certainty of promotion, his noble lineage, and all good attributes he could endow him with.

Priscilla kept at her spinning while this harangue went on, but the drone of the wheel did not prevent her noting a sigh and a catch of the breath that interrupted the discourse now and then. She flushed as she replied, "Why does not Captain Standish come to me himself? If I am worth the winning I ought to be worth the wooing."

But John Alden seemed not to notice the girl's confusion until, in a pause in his eloquence, Priscilla bent her head a little, as if to mend a break in the flax, and said, "Prithee, John, why don't you speak for yourself?"

Then a great light broke on the understanding of John Alden, and a great warmth welled up in his heart, and—they were married. Myles Standish— well, some say that he walked in the wedding procession, while one narrator holds that the sturdy Roundhead tramped away to the woods, where he sat for a day, hating himself, and that he never forgave his *protégé* nor the maiden who took advantage of leap year. However that may be, the wedding was a happy one, and the Aldens of all America claim John and Priscilla for their ancestors.

MOTHER CREWE

MOTHER CREWE was of evil repute in Plymouth in the last century. It was said that she had taken pay for luring a girl into her old farm-house, where a man lay dead of small-pox, with intent to harm her beauty; she was accused of blighting land and driving ships ashore with spells; in brief, she was called a witch, and people, even those who affected to ignore the craft of wizardry, were content to keep away from her. When the Revolution ended, Southward Howland demanded Dame Crewe's house and acre, claiming under law of entail, though primogeniture had been little enforced in America, where there was room and to spare for all. But Howland was stubborn and the woman's house had good situation, so one day he rode to her door and summoned her with a tap of his whip.

" What do you here on my land?" said he.

" I live on land that is my own. I cleared it, built my house here, and no other has claim to it."

" Then I lay claim. The place is mine. I shall tear your cabin down on Friday."

" On Friday they'll dig your grave on Burying Hill. I see the shadow closing round you. You draw it in with every breath. Quick! Home and make your peace!" The hag's withered face was touched with spots of red and her eyes glared in their sunken sockets.

"Bandy no witch words with me, woman. On Friday I will return." And he swung himself into his saddle. As he did so a black cat leaped on Mother Crewe's shoulder and stood there, squalling. The woman listened to its cries as if they were words. Her look of hate deepened. Raising her hand, she cried, "Your day is near its end. Repent!"

"Bah! You have heard what I have said. If on Friday you are not elsewhere, I'll tear the timbers down and bury you in the ruins."

"Enough!" cried the woman, her form straightening, her voice grown shrill. "My curse is on you here and hereafter. Die! Then go down to hell!"

As she said this the cat leaped from her shoulder to the flank of the horse, spitting and clawing, and the frightened steed set off at a furious pace. As he disappeared in the scrub oaks his master was seen vainly trying to stop him. The evening closed in with fog and chill, and before the light waned a man faring homeward came upon the corpse of Southward Howland stretched along the ground.

Myths and Legends

AUNT RACHEL'S CURSE

ON a headland near Plymouth lived "Aunt Rachel," a reputed seer, who made a scant livelihood by forecasting the future for such sea-going people as had crossed her palm. The crew of a certain brig came to see her on the day before sailing, and she reproached one of the lads for keeping bad company. "Avast, there, granny," interrupted another, who took the chiding to himself. "None of your slack, or I'll put a stopper on your gab." The old woman sprang erect. Levelling her skinny finger at the man, she screamed, "Moon cursers! You have set false beacons and wrecked ships for plunder. It was your fathers and mothers who decoyed a brig to these sands and left me child-less and a widow. He who rides the pale horse be your guide, and you be of the number who follow him!"

That night old Rachel's house was burned, and she barely escaped with her life, but when it was time for the brig to sail she took her place among the townfolk who were to see it off. The owner of the brig tried to console her for the loss of the house. "I need it no longer," she answered, "for the narrow house will soon be mine, and you wretches cannot burn that. But you! Who will console you for the loss of your brig?"

"My brig is stanch. She has already passed the worst shoal in the bay."

Tales of Puritan Land

" But she carries a curse. She cannot swim long."

As each successive rock and bar was passed the old woman leaned forward, her hand shaking, her gray locks flying, her eyes starting, her lips mumbling maledictions, " like an evil spirit, chiding forth the storms as ministers of vengeance." The last shoal was passed, the merchant sighed with relief at seeing the vessel now safely on her course, when the woman uttered a harsh cry, and raised her hand as if to command silence until something happened that she evidently expected. For this the onlookers had not long to wait : the brig halted and trembled—her sails shook in the wind, her crew were seen trying to free the cutter—then she careened and sank until only her mast-heads stood out of the water. Most of the company ran for boats and lines, and few saw Rachel pitch forward on the earth—dead, with a fierce smile of exultation on her face. The rescuers came back with all the crew, save one—the man who had challenged the old woman and revengefully burned her cabin. Rachel's body was buried where her house had stood, and the rock—before unknown—where the brig had broken long bore the name of Rachel's Curse.

Myths and Legends

NIX'S MATE

THE black, pyramidal beacon, called Nix's Mate, is well known to yachtsmen, sailors, and excursionists in Boston harbor. It rises above a shoal,—all that is left of a fair, green island which long ago disappeared in the sea. In 1636 it had an extent of twelve acres, and on its highest point was a gallows where pirates were hanged in chains. One night cries were heard on board of a ship that lay at anchor a little way off shore, and when the watch put off, to see what might be amiss, the captain, named Nix, was found murdered in his bed. There was no direct evidence in the case, and no motive could be assigned for the deed, unless it was the expectancy of promotion on the part of the mate, in case of his commander's death.

It was found, however, that this possibility gave significance to certain acts and sayings of that officer during the voyage, and on circumstantial evidence so slight as this he was convicted and sentenced to death. As he was led to execution he swore that he was not guilty, as he had done before, and from the scaffold he cried aloud, " God, show that I am innocent. Let this island sink and prove to these people that I have never stained my hands with human blood." Soon after the execution of his sentence it was noticed that the surf was going higher on the shore, that certain rocks were no longer uncovered at low tide, and in time the island wasted away. The colonists looked with awe on this manifestation and confessed that God had shown their wrong.

THE WILD MAN OF CAPE COD

FOR years after Bellamy's pirate ship was wrecked at Wellfleet, by false pilotage on the part of one of his captives, a strange-looking man used to travel up and down the cape, who was believed to be one of the few survivors of that night of storm, and of the hanging that others underwent after getting ashore. The pirates had money when the ship struck; it was found in the pockets of a hundred drowned who were cast on the beach, as well as among the sands of the cape, for coin was gathered there long after. They supposed the stranger had his share, or more, and that he secreted a quantity of specie near his cabin. After his death gold was found under his clothing in a girdle. He was often received at the houses of the fishermen, both because the people were hospitable and because they feared harm if they refused to feed or shelter him; but if his company grew wearisome he was exorcised by reading aloud a portion of the Bible. When he heard the holy words he invariably departed.

And it was said that fiends came to him at night, for in his room, whether he appeared to sleep or wake, there were groans and blasphemy, uncanny words and sounds that stirred the hair of listeners on their scalps. The unhappy creature cried to be delivered from his tormenters and begged to be spared from seeing a rehearsal of the murders he had committed. For some time he was missed from his haunts, and it was thought that he had secured a ship and set to sea again; but a traveller on the sands, while passing his cabin in the small hours, had heard a more than usual commotion, and could distinguish the voice of the wild man raised in frantic appeal to somebody, or something; still, knowing that it was his habit to cry out so, and having misgivings about approaching the house, the traveller only hurried past. A few neighbors went to the lonely cabin and looked through the windows, which, as well as the doors, were locked on the inside. The wild man lay still and white on the floor, with the furniture upset and pieces of gold clutched in his fingers and scattered about him. There were marks of claws about his neck.

NEWBURY'S OLD ELM

AMONG the venerable relics of Newbury few are better known and more prized than the old elm. It is a stout tree, with a girth of twenty-four and a half feet, and is said to have been standing since 1713. In that year it was planted by Richard Jacques, then a youthful rustic, who had a sweetheart, as all rustics have, and adored her as

Tales of Puritan Land

rustics and other men should do. On one of his visits he stayed uncommonly late. It was nearly ten o'clock when he set off for home. The town had been abed an hour or more; the night was murky and oppressively still, and corpse-candles were dancing in the graveyard. Witch times had not been so far agone that he felt comfortable, and, lest some sprite, bogie, troll, or goblin should waylay him, he tore an elm branch from a tree that grew before his sweetheart's house, and flourished it as he walked. He reached home without experiencing any of the troubles that a superstitious fancy had conjured. As he was about to cast the branch away a comforting vision of his loved one came into his mind, and he determined to plant the branch at his own door, that in the hours of their separation he might be reminded of her who dwelt beneath the parent tree. He did so. It rooted and grew, and when the youth and maid had long been married, their children and grandchildren sported beneath its branches.

SAMUEL SEWALL'S PROPHECY

THE peace of Newbury is deemed to be permanently secured by the prophecy of Samuel Sewall, the young man who married the buxom daughter of Mint-Master John Hull, and received, as wedding portion, her weight in fresh-coined pine-tree shillings. He afterward became notorious as

one of the witchcraft judges. The prophecy has not
been countervailed, nor is it likely to be, whether
the conditions are kept or not. It runs in this wise:

" As long as Plum island shall faithfully keep the
commanded Post, Notwithstanding the hectoring
words and hard blows of the proud and boisterous
ocean ; As long as any Salmon or Sturgeon shall
swim in the streams of Merrimack, or any Perch or
Pickeril in Crane Pond ; As long as the Sea Fowl
shall know the time of their coming, and not neglect
seasonably to visit the places of their acquaintance ;
As long as any Cattel shall be fed with Grass growing in the meadows which doe humbly bow themselves before Turkie Hill ; As long as any Sheep
shall walk upon Old town Hills, and shall from
thence look pleasantly down upon the River Parker
and the fruitful Marishes lying beneath ; As long as
any free and harmless Doves shall find a White Oak
or other Tree within the township to perch or feed,
or build a careless Nest upon, and shall voluntarily
present themselves to perform the office of Gleaners
after Barley Harvest ; As long as Nature shall not
grow old and dote, but shall constantly remember to
give the rows of Indian Corn their education by Pairs
—So long shall Christians be born there and being
first made meet, shall from thence be translated to be
made partakers of the Saints of Light."

Tales of Puritan Land

THE SHRIEKING WOMAN

DURING the latter part of the seventeenth century a Spanish ship, richly laden, was beset off Marblehead by English pirates, who killed every person on board, at the time of the capture, except a beautiful English lady, a passenger on the ship, who was brought ashore at night and brutally murdered at a ledge of rocks near Oakum Bay. As the fishermen who lived near were absent in their boats, the women and children, who were startled from their sleep by her piercing shrieks, dared not attempt a rescue. Taking her a little way from shore in their boat, the pirates flung her into the sea, and as she came to the surface and clutched the gunwale they hewed at her hands with cutlasses. She was heard to cry, "Lord, save me! Mercy! O, Lord Jesus, save me!" Next day the people found her mangled body on the rocks, and, with bitter imprecations at the worse than beasts that had done this wrong, they prepared it for burial. It was interred where it was found, but, although it was committed to the earth with Christian forms, for one hundred and fifty years the victim's cries and appeals were repeated, on each anniversary of the crime, with such distinctness as to affright all who heard them—and most of the citizens of Marblehead claimed to be of that number.

Myths and Legends

AGNES SURRIAGE

WHEN, in 1742, Sir Henry Frankland, collector of the port of Boston, went to Marblehead to inquire into the smuggling that was pretty boldly carried on, he put up at the Fountain Inn. As he entered that hostelry a barefooted girl, of sixteen, who was scrubbing the floor, looked at him. The young man was handsome, well dressed, gallant in bearing, while Agnes Surriage, maid of all work, was of good figure, beautiful face, and modest demeanor. Sir Henry tossed out a coin, bidding her to buy shoes with it, and passed to his room. But the image of Agnes rose constantly before him. He sought her company, found her of ready intelligence for one unschooled, and shortly after this visit he obtained the consent of her parents—humble folk— to take this wild flower to the city and cultivate it.

He gave her such an education as the time and place afforded, dressed her well, and behaved with kindness toward her, while she repaid this care with the frank bestowal of her heart. The result was not foreseen—not intended—but they became as man and wife without having wedded. Colonial society was scandalized, yet the baronet loved the girl sincerely and could not be persuaded to part from her. Having occasion to visit England he took Agnes with him and introduced her as Lady Frankland, but the nature of their alliance had been made known to his relatives and they refused to receive her. The

thought of a permanent union with the girl had not yet presented itself to the young man. An aristocrat could not marry a commoner. A nobleman might destroy the honor of a girl for amusement, but it was beneath his dignity to make reparation for the act.

Sir Henry was called to Portugal in 1755, and Agnes went with him. They arrived inopportunely in one respect, though the sequel showed a blessing in the accident; for while they were sojourning in Lisbon the earthquake occurred that laid the city in ruins and killed sixty thousand people. Sir Henry was in his carriage at the time and was buried beneath a falling wall, but Agnes, who had hurried from her lodging at the first alarm, sped through the rocking streets in search of her lover. She found him at last, and, instead of crying or fainting, she set to work to drag away the stones and timbers that were piled upon him. Had she been a delicate creature, her lover's equal in birth, such as Frankland was used to dance with at the state balls, she could not have done this, but her days of service at the inn had given her a strength that received fresh accessions from hope and love. In an hour she had liberated him, and, carrying him to a place of safety, she cherished the spark of life until health returned. The nobleman had received sufficient proof of Agnes's love and courage. He realized, at last, the superiority of worth to birth. He gave his name, as he had already given his heart, to her, and their married life was happy.

Myths and Legends

FLOOD, FLUID, OR FLOYD IRESON (in some chronicles his name is Benjamin) was making for Marblehead in a furious gale, in the autumn of 1808, in the schooner Betsy. Off Cape Cod he fell in with the schooner Active, of Beverly, in distress, for she had been disabled in the heavy sea and was on her beam ends, at the mercy of the tempest. The master of the Active hailed Ireson and asked to be taken off, for his vessel could not last much longer, but the Betsy, after a parley, laid her course again homeward, leaving the exhausted and despairing crew of the sinking vessel to shift as best they might. The Betsy had not been many hours in port before it was known that men were in peril in the bay, and two crews of volunteers set off instantly to the rescue. But it was too late. The Active was at the bottom of the sea. The captain and three of his men were saved, however, and their grave accusation against the Betsy's skipper was common talk in Marblehead ere many days.

On a moonlight night Flood Ireson was roused by knocking at his door. On opening it he was seized by a band of his townsmen, silently hustled to a deserted spot, stripped, bound, and coated with tar and feathers. At break of day he was pitched into an old dory and dragged along the roads until the bottom of the boat dropped out, when he was mounted in a cart and the procession continued until

Salem was reached. The selectmen of that town turned back the company, and for a part of the way home the cart was drawn by a jeering crowd of fishwives. Ireson was released only when nature had been taxed to the limit of endurance. As his bonds were cut he said, quietly, " I thank you for my ride, gentlemen, but you will live to regret it."

Some of the cooler heads among his fellows have believed the skipper innocent and throw the blame for the abandonment of the sinking vessel on Ireson's mutinous crew. There are others, the universal deniers, who believe that the whole thing is fiction. Those people refuse to believe in their own grandfathers. Ireson became moody and reckless after this adventure. He did not seem to think it worth the attempt to clear himself. At times he seemed trying, by his aggressive acts and bitter speeches, to tempt some hot-tempered townsman to kill him. He died after a severe freezing, having been blown to sea—as some think by his own will —in a smack.

HEARTBREAK HILL

THE name of Heartbreak Hill pertains, in the earliest records of Ipswich, to an eminence in the middle of that town on which there was a large Indian settlement, called Agawam, before the white men settled there and drove the inhabitants out. Ere the English colony had been firmly planted a sailor straying ashore came among the simple natives of Agawam, and finding their ways full of novelty he lived with them for a time. When he found means to return to England he took with him the love of a maiden of the tribe, but the girl herself he left behind, comforting her on his departure with an assurance that before many moons he would return. Months went by and extended into years, and every day the girl climbed Heartbreak Hill to look seaward for some token of her lover. At last a ship was seen trying to make harbor, with a furious gale running her close to shore, where breakers were lashing the rocks and sand. The girl kept her station until the vessel, becoming unmanageable, was hurled against the shore and smashed into a thousand pieces. As its timbers went tossing away on the frothing billows a white, despairing face was lifted to hers for an instant; then it sank and was seen nevermore—her lover's face. The "dusky Ariadne" wasted fast from that day, and she lies buried beside the ledge that was her watch-tower.

END OF VOLUME I.